D1742002

COZUMEL &
THE RIVIERA MAYA

LIZA PRADO & GARY CHANDLER

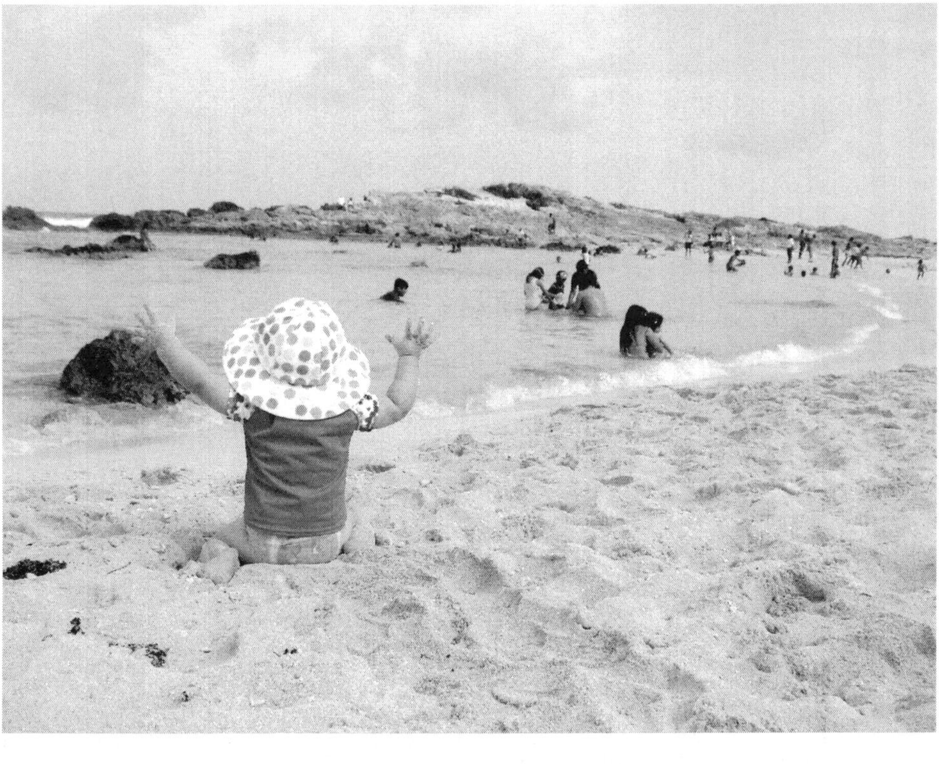

Contents

ISLA COZUMEL &
THE RIVIERA MAYA

ISLA COZUMEL

All around Isla Cozumel, the Caribbean Sea glitters a hundred shades of blue. Beneath the waves, Cozumel's pristine coral reefs make for spectacular diving and snorkeling, the island's number-one draw. San Miguel de Cozumel—usually just called Cozumel, since it's the only city on the island—is where the ferries from Playa del Carmen land. It's also where cruise ships, as many as 10 per day in the high season, arrive; it's then that the waterfront promenade becomes a human river, flowing slowly down a channel of jewelry stores, souvenir shops, and open-air restaurants.

Just a few blocks from the promenade, another Cozumel emerges—a small, friendly community where old folks sit at their windows and dogs sleep in the streets. In spring, masses of orange *framboyán* (poinciana) flowers bloom on shade trees in the plaza, and festivals and religious celebrations are widely attended.

Cozumel's interior—including an important Maya ruin—and its eastern shore are yet another world, lacking even power lines and telephone cables. Heavy surf makes much of the eastern shore too dangerous for swimming, but you easily can spend a day beachcombing or relaxing on the unmanicured beaches and lunching at small restaurants overlooking the sea.

As Mexico's largest island, it shouldn't be surprising to discover that it's so multifaceted. But it's hard not to marvel at how stark the differences are. Come for the diving and snorkeling, but leave time to experience a side of Cozumel you may not have expected.

© LIZA PRADO

HIGHLIGHTS

(Museo de la Isla de Cozumel: Long before Cozumel was a mecca for divers, it was one of the ancient Maya most important religious pilgrimage sites. Soak up the history and ecology of Mexico's largest island at this small but fascinating museum, including dramatic photos from Hurricane Wilma in 2005 (page 12).

(Santa Rosa Wall: Sit back and enjoy the ride at one of Cozumel's marquee dive sites. A strong current whisks you past a long wall, mottled with stony overhangs and gaping caves and home to massive sea fans, translucent sponges, and tropical fish of every size and color (page 13).

(Palancar: With five sections spread over three miles, this massive dive site has something for everyone. Snorkelers can check out Palancar Shallows, while divers can explore the winding ravines and natural arches of Palancar Horseshoe. No matter where you go, you'll enjoy rich coral and vibrant sealife (page 16).

(San Gervasio: Smack dab in the middle of the island, Cozumel's best and biggest Maya ruin is thought to be dedicated to Ixchel, the goddess of fertility; in ancient times, it attracted women from all over the Yucatán seeking her favor (page 16).

(Playa Chen Río: Heavy surf makes most of Cozumel's east side unswimmable, except here, where a rocky arm forms a calm natural pool. Come midweek to have it all to yourself, or on a Sunday to *convivir* (literally, "share life") with local families (page 19).

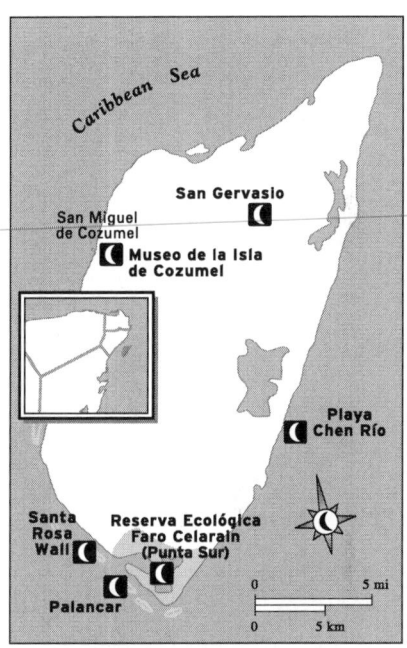

LOOK FOR **(** TO FIND RECOMMENDED SIGHTS, ACTIVITIES, DINING, AND LODGING.

(Reserva Ecológica Faro Celarain (Punta Sur): Snorkel the colorful ocean reef, or stay above water on a catamaran tour of a crocodile-filled lagoon at this scenic nature reserve. Here at the island's southern tip there's also a small museum, ancient Maya lighthouse, and plenty of room to relax on the sand (page 26).

HISTORY

Cozumel has been inhabited since 300 B.C. and was one of three major Maya pilgrimage sites in the region (the others were Chichén Itzá and Izamal in Yucatán state). The name is derived from the island's Maya name, *Cuzamil* (Land of Swallows). The height of its pre-Hispanic occupation was A.D. 1250–1500, when Putún people (also known as the Chontol or Itzás, the same group who built Chichén Itzá's most famous structures) dominated the region as seafaring merchants. Capitan Don Juan de Grijalva arrived on the island in 1518 and dubbed it Isla de Santa Cruz, marking the beginning of the brutal dislocation of the native people by Spanish explorers and conquistadors.

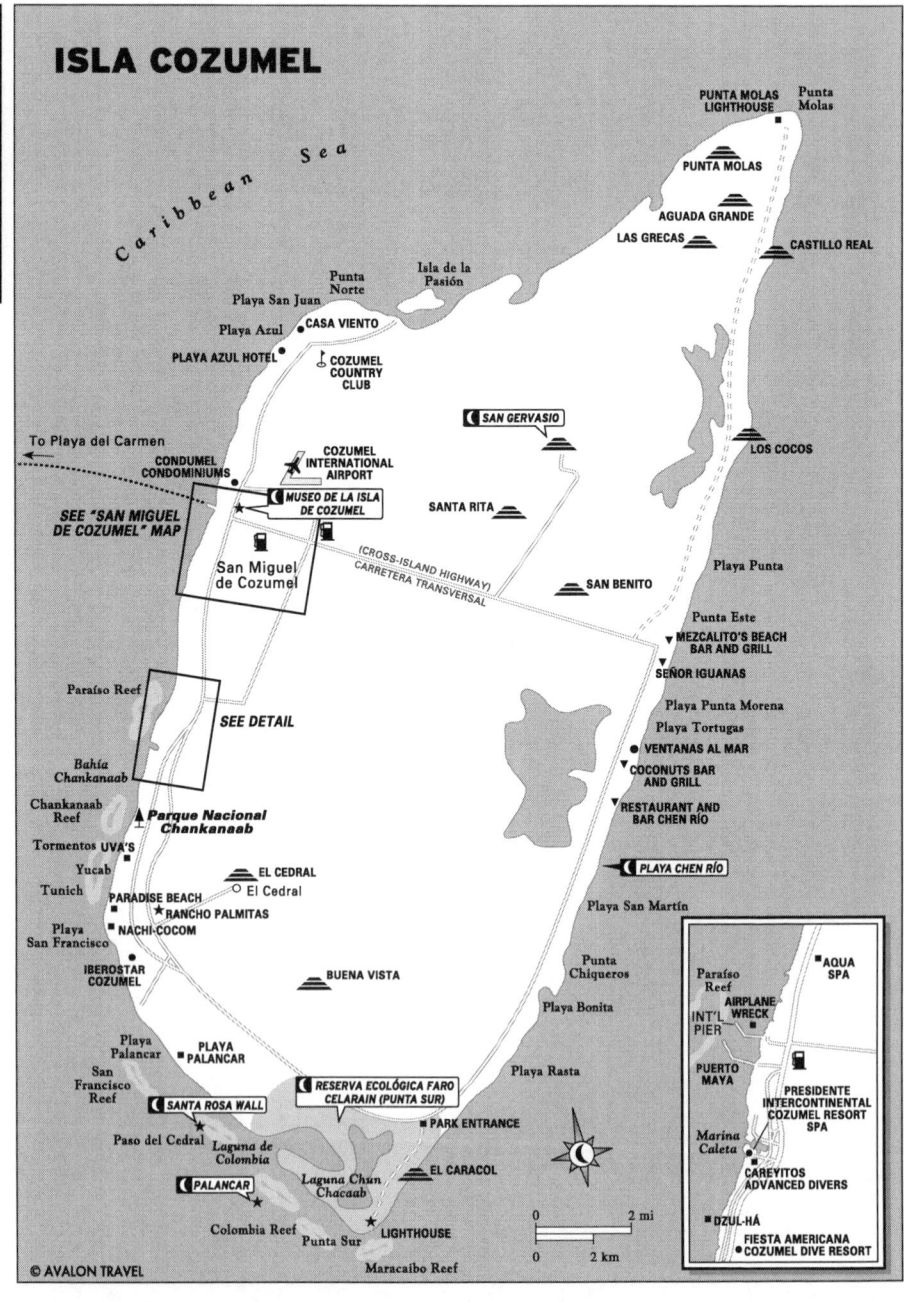

ISLA COZUMEL

PUNTA MOLAS LIGHTHOUSE
Punta Molas

Caribbean Sea

PUNTA MOLAS

AGUADA GRANDE

LAS GRECAS

CASTILLO REAL

Isla de la Pasión

Punta Norte

Playa San Juan

Playa Azul

CASA VIENTO

PLAYA AZUL HOTEL

COZUMEL COUNTRY CLUB

SAN GERVASIO

LOS COCOS

To Playa del Carmen

COZUMEL INTERNATIONAL AIRPORT

CONDUMEL CONDOMINIUMS

MUSEO DE LA ISLA DE COZUMEL

SANTA RITA

SEE "SAN MIGUEL DE COZUMEL" MAP

San Miguel de Cozumel

(CROSS-ISLAND HIGHWAY)
CARRETERA TRANSVERSAL

SAN BENITO

Playa Punta

Punta Este

MEZCALITO'S BEACH BAR AND GRILL

SEÑOR IGUANAS

Paraíso Reef

Playa Punta Morena

Playa Tortugas

SEE DETAIL

VENTANAS AL MAR

COCONUTS BAR AND GRILL

Bahía Chankanaab

RESTAURANT AND BAR CHEN RÍO

Chankanaab Reef

Parque Nacional Chankanaab

Tormentos UVA'S

Yucab

PLAYA CHEN RÍO

Tunich

EL CEDRAL

Playa San Martín

PARADISE BEACH

El Cedral

RANCHO PALMITAS

Playa San Francisco

NACHI-COCOM

IBEROSTAR COZUMEL

BUENA VISTA

Punta Chiqueros

Playa Bonita

Playa Palancar

PLAYA PALANCAR

San Francisco Reef

Playa Rasta

RESERVA ECOLÓGICA FARO CELARAIN (PUNTA SUR)

SANTA ROSA WALL

Paso del Cedral

Laguna de Colombia

PARK ENTRANCE

PALANCAR

Laguna Chun Chacaab

EL CARACOL

Colombia Reef

Punta Sur

LIGHTHOUSE

Maracaibo Reef

0   2 mi

0   2 km

Inset (detail)

Paraíso Reef

AQUA SPA

INT'L PIER

AIRPLANE WRECK

PUERTO MAYA

PRESIDENTE INTERCONTINENTAL COZUMEL RESORT SPA

Marina Caleta

CAREYITOS ADVANCED DIVERS

DZUL-HÁ

FIESTA AMERICANA COZUMEL DIVE RESORT

© AVALON TRAVEL

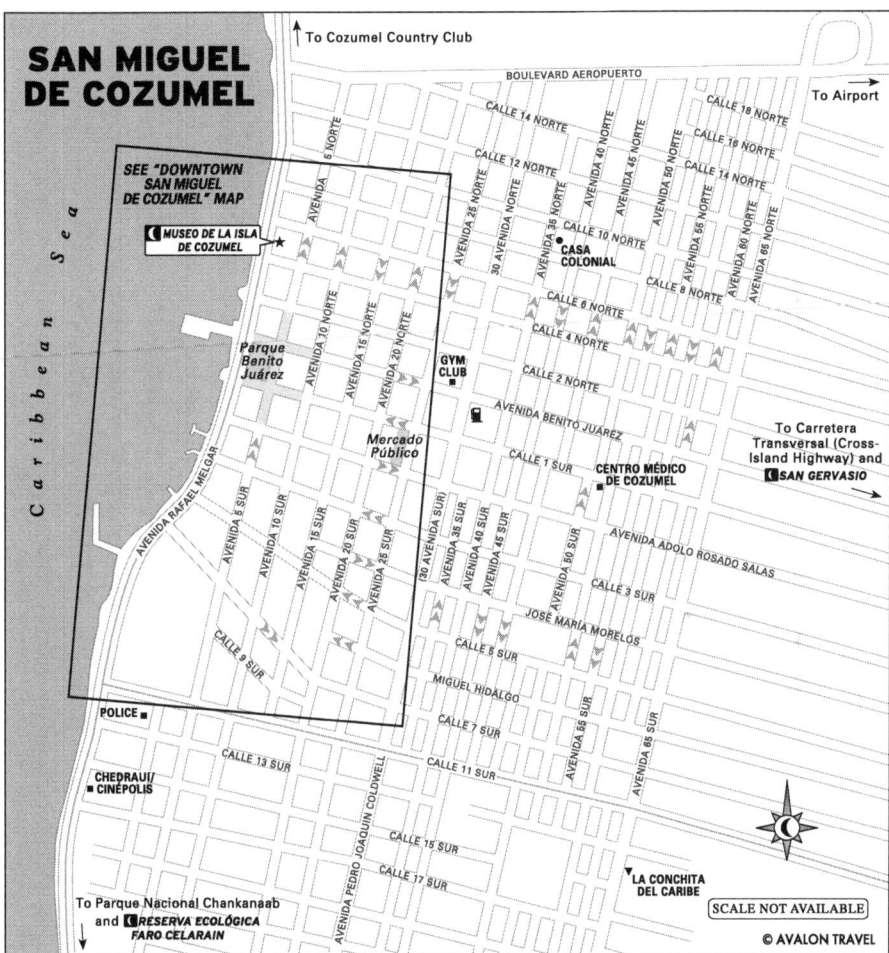

SAN MIGUEL DE COZUMEL

To Cozumel Country Club

BOULEVARD AEROPUERTO

To Airport

Caribbean Sea

SEE "DOWNTOWN
SAN MIGUEL
DE COZUMEL" MAP

MUSEO DE LA ISLA
DE COZUMEL

CASA
COLONIAL

CALLE 14 NORTE
CALLE 12 NORTE
CALLE 18 NORTE
CALLE 16 NORTE
CALLE 14 NORTE
CALLE 10 NORTE
CALLE 8 NORTE
CALLE 6 NORTE
CALLE 4 NORTE
CALLE 2 NORTE

6 NORTE
AVENIDA
25 NORTE
30 AVENIDA NORTE
35 NORTE
AVENIDA 40 NORTE
AVENIDA 45 NORTE
AVENIDA 50 NORTE
AVENIDA 55 NORTE
AVENIDA 60 NORTE
AVENIDA 65 NORTE

Parque
Benito
Juárez

AVENIDA 10 NORTE
AVENIDA 15 NORTE
AVENIDA 20 NORTE

GYM
CLUB

AVENIDA BENITO JUÁREZ

To Carretera
Transversal (Cross-
Island Highway) and
SAN GERVASIO

Mercado
Público

CALLE 1 SUR

CENTRO MÉDICO
DE COZUMEL

AVENIDA RAFAEL MELGAR

AVENIDA 5 SUR
AVENIDA 10 SUR
AVENIDA 15 SUR
AVENIDA 20 SUR
AVENIDA 25 SUR
30 AVENIDA SUR
AVENIDA 35 SUR
AVENIDA 40 SUR
AVENIDA 45 SUR
AVENIDA 50 SUR

AVENIDA ADOLO ROSADO SALAS

CALLE 3 SUR

JOSÉ MARÍA MORELOS

CALLE 5 SUR

CALLE 9 SUR

MIGUEL HIDALGO

POLICE

CALLE 7 SUR

AVENIDA 55 SUR
AVENIDA 65 SUR

CHEDRAUI/
CINÉPOLIS

CALLE 13 SUR

CALLE 11 SUR

AVENIDA PEDRO JOAQUÍN COLDWELL

CALLE 15 SUR

CALLE 17 SUR

LA CONCHITA
DEL CARIBE

To Parque Nacional Chankanaab
and RESERVA ECOLÓGICA
FARO CELARAIN

SCALE NOT AVAILABLE

© AVALON TRAVEL

It eventually was overrun by British and Dutch pirates who used it as a base of operations. By the mid-1800s, however, the island was virtually uninhabited. The henequen, chicle, and coconut-oil booms attracted a new wave of people to the Quintana Roo territory (it didn't become a state until 1974) and Cozumel slowly rebounded, this time with a mostly Mexican mestizo population.

Cozumel's reputation as a world-class diving and tourist destination can be traced to Jacques Cousteau's enthusiastic and widely viewed programs about Cozumel's reefs in 1959, and of course the establishment of Cancún in the 1970s.

PLANNING YOUR TIME

Don't let the cruise ship hubbub on Avenida Rafael Melgar turn you off from the town altogether. Besides the fact that most of the hotels, dive shops, banks, and other services are here, the town itself has much to offer, including a pleasant central plaza and a great museum. Budget a day or two to rent a car and explore the rest of the island, including the beach clubs, Maya ruins, family-friendly ecoparks, and the wild beaches and deserted coastline of Cozumel's eastern side.

ORIENTATION

The town of San Miguel de Cozumel is located on the west side of the island. The main passenger ferry lands here, across from the central plaza. Most streets are one-way in town; if you're driving, be aware that *avenidas* (avenues) run north–south and have the right-of-way over *calles* (streets), which run east–west. Once you leave town, there is a single road that circles the entire island.

Avenida Benito Juárez is one of the main streets in San Miguel de Cozumel, beginning at the central plaza, crossing town, and becoming the Carretera Transversal (Cross-Island Highway). The highway passes the turnoff to the San Gervasio ruins before intersecting with the coastal road. The coastal road follows Cozumel's eastern shore, which is dotted with a few beach clubs and restaurants. Rounding the southern tip, the road heads north along the west shore before becoming Avenida Rafael Melgar and returning to the central plaza. Continuing north, the road passes turnoffs to the airport and a country club before turning to dirt and eventually dead-ending.

Sights

PARQUE BENITO JUÁREZ

Cozumel's central plaza is surprisingly peaceful considering the mass of humanity that disembarks at the ferry pier directly across the street, and from cruise ship ports just down the road. Few foreign visitors take time to linger in the park itself, which has freshly painted benches, tree-filled planters, a boxy clock tower, and busts of late Mexican president Benito Juárez and General Andrés Quintana Roo. The city municipal building, occupying most of the plaza's east side, was beautifully restored following Hurricane Wilma in 2005, with an airy commercial center on the ground floor and civic offices above. And though the central plaza is smack in the middle of Cozumel's tourist corridor, it is still a place local families come to stroll about, especially evenings and weekends, when live bands sometimes play in the central gazebo, and balloon and cotton candy vendors do a brisk trade.

◖ MUSEO DE LA ISLA DE COZUMEL

The town's small but excellent museum (Av. Rafael Melgar at Calle 6, tel. 987/872-1434, 9 A.M.–5 P.M. Mon.–Sat., 9 A.M.–4 P.M. Sun., US$3) is on the waterfront in what was once a turn-of-the-20th-century hotel. Well-composed exhibits in English and Spanish describe the island's wildlife, coral reefs, and the fascinating, sometimes tortured history of human presence here, from the Maya pilgrims who came to worship the fertility goddess to present-day survivors of devastating hurricanes. Be sure to visit in the morning if you want to avoid the cruise ship crowds. The museum also has a small bookstore, a library, and a pleasant outdoor café overlooking the sea.

CORAL REEFS

Cozumel's coral reef—and the world-class diving and snorkeling it provides—is the main reason people come to the island. The reef was designated a national marine reserve more than two decades ago, and the waters have thrived under the park's rigorous protection and cleanup programs. In 2005, Hurricane Wilma took a major toll on the reef, snapping off coral and sponges with its powerful surge, and leaving other sections smothered under a thick layer of sand and debris. But hurricanes are nothing new to Cozumel or its coral, and reports of vast damage to the reef were greatly exaggerated. Cozumel's underwater treasure remains very much alive, supporting a plethora of creatures, its seascapes as stunning as ever. Dozens of dive and snorkeling sites encircle the island, and the 1,000-meter-deep (3,281-foot) channel between Cozumel and the mainland still provides spectacular drift and wall dives. Here is a list of some of the most popular dives, though by no means all of the worthwhile ones.

Airplane Wreck

A 40-passenger Convair airliner lies on Cozumel's seabed, about 65 meters (195 feet) from the shore near the El Cid hotel. Sunk in 1977 for the Mexican movie production of *Survive II,* the plane has been broken into pieces and strewn about the site by years of storms. The site itself is relatively flat, though with parrot fish, damselfish, and a host of sea fans and small coral heads, there's plenty to see. With depth ranges of 3–15 meters (9–45 feet), this is a good site for snorkelers too.

Paraíso

Just south of the international pier, and about 200 meters (656 feet) from shore, lies Paraíso, an impressive two-lane coral ridge. Medium-size coral—mostly brain and star—attract French and gray angelfish, squirrel fish, and sea cucumbers. This site is also popular for night dives because of its proximity to hotels, which means less time on the boat. Depth ranges 11–15 meters (33–45 feet). Snorkeling is decent near the shore but be very careful of boat traffic.

Dzul-Há (aka The Money Bar)

Located off the old coastal road (Km. 6.5), Dzul-Há is one of the best spots for snorkeling from shore, with small coral heads and sea fans that support a colorful array of fish like blue tangs, parrot fish, and queen angels. Steps lead into the ocean, where depths range 3–10 meters (10–30 feet). You can rent snorkel gear on-site for US$10.

Tormentos

At this site divers can see about 60 coral heads, each decorated with an assortment of sea fans, brain and whip corals, and sponges.

Invertebrates like to hide out in the host of crevices—look for flamingo tongue shells, arrow crabs, and black crinoids. Lobster and nurse sharks like the scene too—keep your eyes peeled for them, especially at the north end of the site. Depth ranges 10–20 meters (30–60 feet). The site is popular with photographers.

Yucab

A perfect drift dive, Yucab has archways, overhangs, and large coral heads—some as tall as three meters (10 feet)—that are alive with an incredible array of creatures: Lobsters, banded coral shrimp, butterfly fish, and angelfish can almost always be found here. Videographers typically have a field day. Depth ranges 12–20 meters (36–60 feet).

Tunich

Tunich usually has a 1.5-knot current, which makes it an excellent high-velocity drift dive. The site itself has a white-sand bottom with a gentle downward slope that ends in a drop-off. Along the way, the reef is dotted with basket sponges and intricately textured corals. Divers regularly encounter turtles, eagle rays, moray eels, bar jacks, and parrot fish. The depth ranges 15–30 meters (45–90 feet).

◖ Santa Rosa Wall

With a sensational drop-off that begins at 22 meters (72.2 feet), this spectacular site is known for its tunnels, caves, and stony overhangs. Teeming with sealife, it's home to translucent sponges, mammoth sea fans, file clams, blennies, fairy basslets, gray angelfish, and groupers. Strong currents make this a good drift dive, especially for experienced divers. Depth ranges 10–30 meters (30–90 feet).

Paso del Cedral

A strip reef lined with small corals like disk and cactus, this site attracts large schools of fish like blue striped grunts and snapper—perfect for dramatic photographs. Southern stingrays often are seen gliding over the sandy areas just inside the reef. Depths range 10–20 meters (30–60 feet).

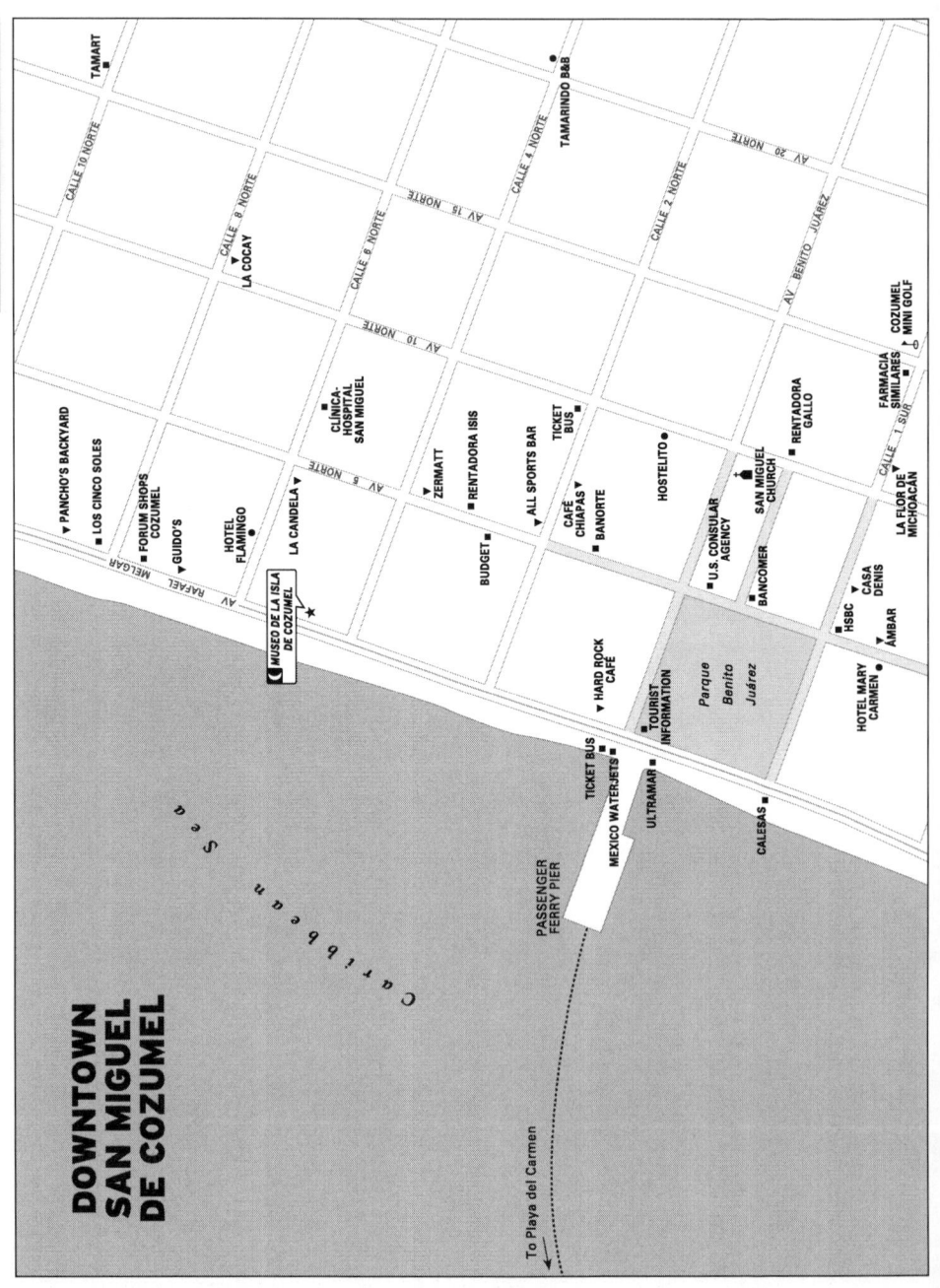

DOWNTOWN
SAN MIGUEL
DE COZUMEL

To Playa del Carmen

Caribbean Sea

PASSENGER
FERRY PIER

TICKET BUS
MEXICO WATERJETS
ULTRAMAR
CALEXAS

TOURIST
INFORMATION

HARD ROCK
CAFÉ

Parque
Benito
Juárez

HOTEL MARY
CARMEN

U.S. CONSULAR
AGENCY

SAN MIGUEL
CHURCH

BANCOMER

HSBC

CASA
DENIS

AMBAR

LA FLOR DE
MICHOACÁN

HOSTELITO

RENTADORA
GALLO

FARMACIA
SIMILARES

COZUMEL
MINI GOLF

CALLE 1 SUR

AV. BENITO JUÁREZ

CAFÉ
CHIAPAS

BANORTE

TICKET
BUS

ALL SPORTS BAR

RENTADORA ISIS

ZERMATT

BUDGET

AV 5 NORTE

LA CANDELA

HOTEL
FLAMINGO

GUIDO'S

FORUM SHOPS
COZUMEL

LOS CINCO SOLES

PANCHO'S BACKYARD

AV RAFAEL E. MELGAR

MUSEO DE LA ISLA
DE COZUMEL

CLINICA-
HOSPITAL
SAN MIGUEL

AV 10 NORTE

CALLE 8 NORTE

LA COCAY

CALLE 6 NORTE

CALLE 8 NORTE

AV 15 NORTE

AV 20 NORTE

CALLE 2 NORTE

CALLE 4 NORTE

TAMARINDO B&B

TAMART

CALLE 10 NORTE

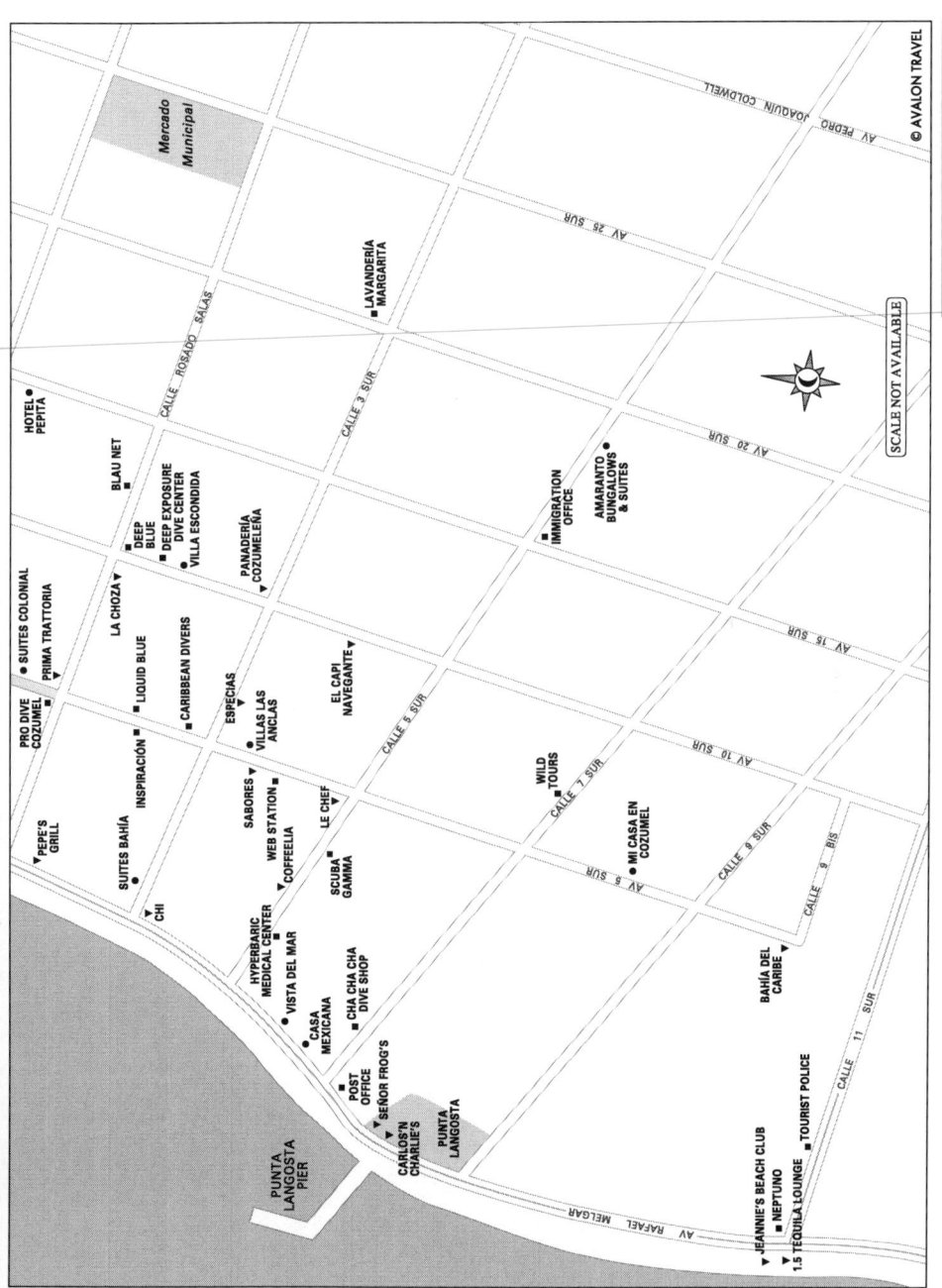

© AVALON TRAVEL

SCALE NOT AVAILABLE

Mercado Municipal

AV PEDRO JOAQUIN COLDWELL

AV 25 SUR

CALLE ROSADO SALAS

LAVANDERÍA MARGARITA

CALLE 3 SUR

AV 20 SUR

HOTEL PEPITA

BLAU NET

DEEP BLUE

DEEP EXPOSURE DIVE CENTER

VILLA ESCONDIDA

PANADERÍA COZUMELEÑA

IMMIGRATION OFFICE

AMARANTO BUNGALOWS & SUITES

SUITES COLONIAL

PRIMA TRATTORIA

LA CHOZA

LIQUID BLUE

CARIBBEAN DIVERS

ESPECIAS

VILLAS LAS ANCLAS

EL CAPI NAVEGANTE

CALLE 5 SUR

AV 15 SUR

PRO DIVE COZUMEL

INSPIRACION

SABORES

WEB STATION

LE CHEF

WILD TOURS

CALLE 7 SUR

AV 10 SUR

PEPE'S GRILL

SUITES BAHIA

CHI

HYPERBARIC MEDICAL CENTER

COFFEELIA

SCUBA GAMMA

MI CASA EN COZUMEL

CALLE 9 SUR

CALLE 9 BIS

AV 5 SUR

VISTA DEL MAR

CASA MEXICANA

CHA CHA DIVE SHOP

BAHÍA DEL CARIBE

POST OFFICE

SEÑOR FROG'S

PUNTA LANGOSTA PIER

CARLOS'N CHARLIE'S

PUNTA LANGOSTA

JEANNIE'S BEACH CLUB

NEPTUNO

1.5 TEQUILA LOUNGE

TOURIST POLICE

CALLE 11 SUR

AV RAFAEL MELGAR

◖ Palancar

This spectacular five-kilometer-long (3.1-mile) dive spot is actually made up of five different sites—Shallows, Garden, Horseshoe, Caves, and Deep. It is known for its series of enormous coral buttresses. Some drop off dramatically into winding ravines, deep canyons, and passageways; others have become archways and tunnels with formations 15 meters (49.2 feet) tall. The most popular site here is Palancar Horseshoe, which is made up of a horseshoe-shaped series of coral heads at the top of a drop-off. All the sites, however, are teeming with reef life. Palancar ranges in depth 10–40 meters (30–120 feet).

Colombia

An enormous coral buttress, Colombia boasts tall coral pillars separated by passageways, channels, and ravines. Divers enjoy drifting past huge sponges, anemones, and swaying sea fans. Larger creatures—sea turtles, groupers, and spotted eagle rays—are commonly seen here. This drift dive is recommended for experienced divers. Depths range 10–40 meters (30–120 feet).

Maracaibo

At the island's southern tip, Maracaibo is a deep buttress reef interspersed with tunnels, caves, and vertical walls. It is known for its immense coral formations as well as its large animals—sharks (blacktips, hammerheads, tigers, and bulls) and schools of manta and eagle rays. A deep-drift dive, this site is recommended for advanced divers only. Depths range 30–40 meters (90–120 feet) and up.

ARCHAEOLOGICAL ZONES

Isla Cozumel played a deeply significant role in the Maya world as an important port of trade and, more importantly, as one of three major destinations of religious pilgrimages (the others were Izamal and Chichén Itzá, both in Yucatán state). The island's primary site—known as San Gervasio today—was dedicated to Ixchel (Lady Rainbow), the Maya goddess of fertility as well as of the moon, childbirth, medicine,

and weaving. Archaeologists believe that every Maya woman was expected, at least once in her lifetime, to journey to Cozumel to make offerings to Ixchel for fertility—her own, and that of her family's fields. Cozumel's draw was powerful, as inscriptions there refer to places and events hundreds of miles away.

Twenty-four archaeological sites have been discovered on the island, though only four are easily accessible, and only the largest—San Gervasio—can properly be called a tourist attraction. San Gervasio is certainly not as glorious as ruins found on the mainland, but it's well worth a visit all the same.

◖ San Gervasio

The area around San Gervasio (Cross-Island Hwy. Km. 7.5, www.cozumelparks.com, 7 A.M.–4 P.M. daily, US$7) was populated as early as A.D. 200, and remained so after the general Maya collapse (A.D. 800–900) and well into the Spanish conquest. In fact, archaeologists excavating the ruins found a crypt containing 50 skeletons along with numerous Spanish beads; the bodies are thought to be those of 16th-century Maya who died from diseases brought by the conquistadors.

Today's visitors will find a modest ruin, whose small square buildings with short doors are typical of those found elsewhere on the island. This style, known as *oratorio,* almost certainly developed in response to climatic imperatives: Anything built here needed to withstand the hurricanes that have pummeled Cozumel for millennia. (Sure enough, Hurricane Wilma did no major damage to San Gervasio's structures.)

San Gervasio has three building groups that are accessible to the public—Las Manitas, Central Plaza, and Murciélagos; all are connected by trails that follow the same ancient causeways used by the city's original inhabitants. A fourth building group—El Ramonal—is not yet open to the public.

Entering the site, you'll come first to the building group named after the structure **Las Manitas** (Little Hands) for the red handprints still visible on one of its walls. This structure

© LIZA PRADO

Cozumel's largest and most important ruin was dedicated to Ixchel, the goddess of fertility.

is thought to have been the home of one of San Gervasio's kings, Ah Huneb Itza, and the inner temple was likely a personal sanctuary. Just east of the Las Manitas building is **Chi Chan Nah;** consisting of two rooms, it is the smallest structure in San Gervasio. The exact purpose of this building is unknown, though it is theorized that it was used for rituals.

Bearing left, the trail leads to the **Central Plaza,** a large courtyard surrounded by nine low structures in various states of decay; it is believed that the structures were made taller with wood extensions. The Plaza Central served as the seat of power in San Gervasio's latest era, from A.D. 1200 onward. At the northwest side of the Plaza Central is the somewhat precarious-looking **El Arco** (The Arch), which served as an entrance to this section of the city.

At 0.5 kilometer (0.3 mile) from the Plaza Central is the **Murciélagos** (Bats) building group, containing the site's largest and most important structure: Ka'na Nah (Tall House). Also dating to San Gervasio's later era, this was the temple of the goddess Ixchel, and in its heyday would have been covered in stucco and painted red, blue, green, and black.

Finally, on the northeastern edge of San Gervasio rests **Nohoch Nah** (Big House), a boxy but serene temple. With an interior altar, the temple might have been used by religious pilgrims to make an offering upon entering or leaving San Gervasio. It was originally covered in stucco and painted a multitude of colors.

Guides can be hired at the visitors center for a fixed rate: US$20 for a one-hour tour in Spanish, English, French, or German. Prices are per group, which can include up to six people. Tips are customary and are not included in the price.

El Cedral

South of town and just beyond Playa San Francisco, a paved turnoff leads to El Cedral (8 A.M.–5 P.M. daily, free), the oldest Maya structure on the island. Once the hub of Maya life on the island, it is the first Maya site that the Spaniards stumbled upon in 1518; allegedly, the first Catholic mass in Mexico was held here. Today the site is small and underwhelming, though it still bears a few traces of the original paint and stucco. (It's amazing that these remnants are left, despite the passage of time—and its use as a jail in the 1800s.) The ruin is located in the like-named village of El Cedral; tour operators often bring visitors here to wander about and buy handicrafts.

El Caracol

Located inside the Reserva Ecológica Faro Celarain, El Caracol is a small conch-shaped structure that dates to A.D. 1200. It's believed to have been a lighthouse, where Maya used smoke and flames to lead boats to safety. Small openings at the top of the structure also acted as whistles to alert Maya to approaching tropical storms and hurricanes. Admission to the reserve includes access to this small site.

Castillo Real

Castillo Real is a partially excavated site with a temple, two chambers, and a lookout tower. It is believed to have been a Maya watchtower to protect against approaching enemies. It's located on the northeastern side of the island, on the sand road to Punta Molas. Unfortunately, this area has been closed to the public for several years, ostensibly to protect the mangroves, but also due to a land dispute involving some of the island's political heavyweights. Hopefully it will be reopened by the time you read this… but don't hold your breath.

BEACHES AND BEACH CLUBS

Cozumel isn't famous for its beaches, but it is not without a few beautiful stretches of sand. A series of beach clubs on the calmer west side are the best places to enjoy the sun and sand, but they can get crowded. Beaches on the east side are windy and picturesque, and the surf can be fierce.

Western Cozumel

PLAYA PALANCAR

On the west side of the island with calm turquoise waters, a small beach, and lots of coconut trees, Playa Palancar (Km. 19.5, no phone, 9 A.M.–5 P.M. daily) caters to visitors who just

want to spend a quiet day lounging in a hammock or snorkeling in the nearby Palancar reef. A *palapa*-roofed restaurant serves classic Mexican seafood and a wide range of drinks (US$5–16). Trips to the reef leave as soon as there is a critical mass of people (snorkel US$30, 1.5 hours, scuba US$80/two tanks). Snorkel gear also can be rented separately (US$10), but with no reef within striking distance, there's not much point in spending your cash on it. The club is 750 meters (0.5 mile) down a dirt road from the central road.

PLAYA SAN FRANCISCO

With over three kilometers (1.9 miles) of thick white sand and calm turquoise waters, Playa San Francisco is one of Cozumel's most attractive beaches. Its beauty is compromised somewhat—to say nothing of the tranquility—by a string of beach clubs. Two of the most attractive are **Nachi-Cocom** (Carr. Costera Sur Km. 16.5, tel. 987/872-1811, www.cozumelnachicocom.net, 9 A.M.–5 P.M. daily) and **Paradise Beach** (Carr. Costera Sur Km. 14.5, tel. 987/871-9010, www.paradise-beach-cozumel.com, 9 A.M.–sunset daily). Neither charge cover, but visitors must spend at least US$10 on food and drinks to be able to use the beach chairs and umbrellas. At Paradise Beach, an additional US$10 gets you unlimited use of kayaks, snorkel gear, beach floats, and other beach gear. Both places typically are hopping with cruise-shippers, though Nachi-Cocom tends to be rowdier, with scantily clad visitors piled into the whirlpool tub. The sand and sea are gorgeous all the same at both places, and the din evaporates just a hundred meters down the beach if you want a quiet place to lay out your towel and catch up on backlogged *New Yorkers*.

Uva's (Carr. Costera Sur Km. 8.5, tel. 987/800-9806, 8 A.M.–5 P.M. Mon.–Sat., US$7 cover, US$59 all-inclusive) oozes cool, with minimalist furnishings and mellow beats, plus a small clean pool and a nice patch of beach. Visitors can rent snorkel gear (US$15) as well as clear acrylic kayaks (aka "dry snorkeling," US$40). Or opt instead for an all-inclusive day pass that includes the gear rentals, a 45-minute snorkel tour, lunch, and open bar.

Eastern Cozumel

On the east side of the island you'll find a wild and windswept coastline dotted with beaches facing the open ocean. The surf here can be quite rough and only a few beaches are safe for swimming. The exception is when *nortes* (northern storm fronts) hit the island, and the west side turns choppy while the east side goes perfectly flat.

Right where the Carretera Transversal hits the coast, two low-key restaurants sit alongside each other: **Mezcalito's Beach Bar and Grill** (tel. 987/872-1616, www.mezcalitos.com, 9 A.M.–6 P.M. daily) and **Señor Iguanas** (no phone, 8 A.M.–5 P.M. Mon.–Sat., 9 A.M.–5 P.M. Sun.). Both have similar menus (ceviche, fried fish, hamburgers, US$7–14), drinks (beer, margaritas, and tequila shots, US$2.50–5), and services (beachside chairs, hammocks, and *palapas,* free if you buy something from the restaurant). If you're feeling brave and have experience in rough waters, rent a boogie board from Señor Iguanas (US$4/two hrs)—a lot of fun if you can handle the surf.

PLAYA TORTUGAS

About six kilometers (3.7 miles) south of the Carretera Transversal intersection is Playa Tortugas, a broad beautiful beach on the north side of the Ventanas al Mar hotel. The scenic windswept beach is good for surfing—and has nesting turtles from May to November—but it is often too rough for swimming or snorkeling. Still, it makes a good place to watch the wild and crashing waves anytime.

A few steps away is **Coconuts Bar and Grill** (10:30 A.M.–sunset daily, US$5–13). Set on a magnificent bluff, tables and chairs are arranged so that patrons can enjoy the glorious views of the beach below and the Caribbean beyond. Coconuts serves classic beach fare—nachos, ceviche, tacos—that goes great with a cold beer.

◖ PLAYA CHEN RÍO

The best place to swim on the east side of the island is Playa Chen Río (1 km/0.6 mi

© LIZA PRADO

Playa Chen Río is protected by a long rocky spit, making it the east side's best place for swimming.

south of Coconuts Bar), where a rocky spit blocks the waves, forming a huge natural pool, and lifeguards are on duty on weekends. Quiet during the week, it's lively and bustling most Sundays, when local families turn out in force. **Restaurant and Bar Chen Río** (11 A.M.–6 P.M. daily, US$12–26) is located here, but the food is so expensive most people just bring a picnic.

PLAYA BONITA

Three kilometers farther south, Playa Bonita is another picturesque curve of sand with plenty of room to lay out a towel and soak in the sun. Heavy surf usually makes swimming here inadvisable, but it's definitely dramatic. A small **beach restaurant** (10 A.M.–5 P.M. daily) serves hamburgers, fresh fish, and other standards at decent prices.

PLAYA RASTA

Playa Rasta is the last beach you hit before turning west on the highway. It's mostly a rocky stretch of beach with a few sandy inlets and two restaurants blasting reggae at each other. It's not really the best place to spend the day—unless you like rambling on rocks and have a serious craving for jerk chicken.

Northeastern Cozumel

Cozumel's northeastern shoulder is its lost coast, the wildest and least-visited part of the island. Paved roads hug (or give access to) almost every part of the island's shoreline, save

that 25-kilometer (15-mile) stretch from the Carretera Transversal up to Punta Molas. A rutted sand road has long been the only access route, but it was severely damaged in 2005 by Hurricane Wilma. For the last several years the area has been closed to the public entirely, ostensibly over concerns for protected mangroves there, but in fact more closely related to political machinations surrounding a huge and hotly disputed development project planned there.

The northeast coast surely will reopen—hopefully by the time you read this—and travelers will once again be able to explore this isolated and windswept part of the island. When it's open, one way to visit is by joining an ATV tour, which is a popular option with cruise ship passengers. More adventurous visitors can rent a jeep or even hike in, camping on the beach along the way. (If you're considering driving a rental car, double-check that the insurance policy covers off-roading.) The first beaches you hit are nice beachcombing spots, and are good places to pitch a tent. About 22 kilometers (14 miles) north, you'll pass the Maya site of **Castillo Real** and farther on is the **Punta Molas Lighthouse,** marking the northeasternmost tip of the island.

Whatever your means of transportation, don't come alone or unprepared. There are no facilities whatsoever, nor any other people most of the time. If you plan to camp, take plenty of water and food, a flashlight, extra batteries, bug repellent, and a mosquito net.

Entertainment and Shopping

NIGHTLIFE
Nightclubs
A classic Cozumeleño nightclub, **Neptuno** (Av. Rafael Melgar at Calle 11, tel. 987/872-4374, 9 P.M.–4 A.M. Tues.–Sun., cover varies) is a good place to check out the local party scene. It has a large dance floor—check out the old-school lighting and disco ball—where revelers bump and grind to reggae, house, techno, and Latin beats. Things really get going after midnight.

Bars
The hottest spot in town, **1.5 Tequila Lounge** (Av. Rafael Melgar at Calle 11, tel. 987/872-4421, 9 P.M.–4 A.M. Mon.–Sat., US$4.75 cover) is a hip urban lounge bar overlooking the Caribbean. It has low couches and chairs, outdoor decks, and cool fusion jazz playing in the background. Specialty shooters are the way to go, with an order of sashimi as a chaser.

Ámbar (Av. 5 btwn. Calles 1 and Rosado Salas, tel. 987/869-1955, 11 A.M.–midnight Mon.–Thurs., 11 A.M.–2 A.M. Fri.–Sat., 5–11 P.M. Sun.) is another go-to bar on Friday and Saturday nights. Billowing white fabrics, dim lighting, modern white furniture, and a DJ spinning jazz, funk, and house make this a popular spot. There's also an outdoor lounge, which is especially nice on warm nights.

If you're dying to catch the big game on a big screen (or at least a bunch of little ones), check out **All Sports Bar** (Calle 2 at Av. 5 Norte, tel. 987/869-2246, 10 A.M.–11 P.M. Mon.–Thurs., 10–3 A.M. Fri.–Sun.). It's not the most charming place, but then again it's all about the TVs.

For a spring break atmosphere all day (and all year) long, head to the Punta Langosta shopping center, where **Carlos 'n Charlie's** (tel. 987/869-1648, 10 A.M.–1:30 A.M. Mon.–Fri., 11 A.M.–1:30 A.M. Sat., 5 P.M.–1:30 A.M. Sun.), **Señor Frog's** (tel. 987/869-2246, 8 A.M.–midnight Mon.–Thurs., 8 A.M.–2 A.M. Fri.–Sat.), and the **Hard Rock Café Bar & Gift Shop** (8 A.M.–midnight Mon.–Sat., 10 A.M.–6 P.M.

Sun.) make driving beats, drink specials, and dancing on tables the norm.

THE ARTS
Cultural and Music Performances
Every Sunday evening, the city hosts an **open-air concert** in the central plaza. Locals and expats come out to enjoy the show—put on a clean T-shirt and your nicest flip-flops and you'll fit right in. Concerts typically begin at 7 P.M.

Cinema
You can catch relatively recent movies at **Cinépolis** (Av. Rafael Melgar btwn. Calles 15 and 17, tel. 987/869-0799, US$4–5, US$3 before 3 P.M. and all day Wed.) in the Chedraui shopping center.

FESTIVALS AND EVENTS
Carnaval
Cozumel is one of the few places in Mexico where Carnaval is celebrated with vigor, though the island's one-night celebration is still pretty mellow compared to the weeks or months of partying that mark the holiday elsewhere in the Caribbean and in South America. Held in February, Carnaval in Cozumel centers around a parade of floats and dance troupes, all decked out in colorful dress, masks, and glitter. Entire families come out together to participate and watch. Spectators dance and cheer in the streets as the floats go by, and many join the moving dance party that follows the floats with the largest speakers. Eventually the parade ends up in the center of town, where more music, dancing, and partying continue late into the night.

Festival de El Cedral
Residents of the village of El Cedral celebrate their namesake festival beginning around April 23 and culminating on May 3, the Day of the Holy Cross. Traditionally, the festival entails daily prayer sessions and ends with a dance called the Baile de las Cabezas de Cochino (Dance of the Pigs' Heads). The festival, begun

by a survivor of the Caste War to honor the power of the cross, has morphed over the years into a somewhat more secular affair, with rodeos, dancing, music, and general revelry.

Rodeo de Lanchas Mexicanas

Every May, Cozumel hosts a popular sport fishing tournament known affectionately as the Mexican Boat Rodeo (Av. 20 btw. Calles 13 and 15, 987/872-3701, torneocozumel@ hotmail.com). Anglers from all over Mexico participate—including nearly 200 boats— and international anglers are welcome as long as they register their boats in Mexico. May is when the Gulf Stream draws big game to the waters around Cozumel, including tuna, dorado, marlin, and, sailfish.

SHOPPING

Shopping in Cozumel is aimed straight at cruise ship passengers—and its no wonder, since they tend to spend a lot of money quickly. Avenida Rafael Melgar is where most of the action is, with a succession of marble-floored shops blasting air-conditioning to entice sweaty passersby in for a refreshing look around. Overpriced jewelry, T-shirt, and souvenir shops see the most buyer traffic, although here and there are a few shops worth checking out.

Los Cinco Soles (Av. Rafael Melgar at Calle 8, tel. 987/872-0132, www.loscincosoles.com, 8 A.M.–8 P.M. Mon.–Thurs., 8 A.M.–9 P.M. Fri.–Sat., 10 A.M.–4 P.M. Sun.) has room upon room of impressive Mexican folk art: pre-Columbian replicas, *barro negro* pottery, colorful *rebosos* (shawls), and hand-carved furniture. It's definitely worth a stop, if even just to admire the artisanship. There's a smaller satellite shop at the Punta Langosta mall.

Though pricey, **Pro Dive Cozumel** (Calle Rosado Salas at Av. 5, tel. 987/872-4123,

Carnaval in Cozumel is celebrated with parades and dancing in the streets.

© GARY CHANDLER

www.prodivecozumel.com, 8 A.M.–10 P.M. Mon.–Sat., 9 A.M.–10 P.M. Sun.) has a great selection of snorkel and dive equipment—perfect if you've forgotten your mask or lost a fin. For more options, try the **Cressi** retail shop across the street.

Punta Langosta (Av. Rafael Melgar btwn. Calles 7 and 11, 9 A.M.–8 P.M. daily) is Cozumel's swankiest shopping center. The ultramodern open-air building is home to high-end clothing boutiques, air-conditioned jewelry stores, and fancy ice cream shops.

A small shopping center on the north end of town, **Forum Shops Cozumel** (Av. Rafael Melgar at Calle 8, 8:30 A.M.–5:30 P.M. Mon.–Sat.) is nowhere near as nice as Punta Langosta, but it has a small collection of souvenir shops that are a bit more affordable.

Sports and Recreation

SCUBA DIVING

Cozumel is considered one the world's best places to scuba dive, which is the best and most popular reason to visit the island. Not surprisingly, Cozumel has a profusion of dive shops and operators—more than 100 at last count. Rates are relatively uniform across the island: for fun diving, expect to pay US$65–80 for a two-tank dive, plus US$10–20 for equipment rental, if you need it, while PADI open-water certification courses run US$350–400 (3–4 days, including all equipment and materials). Virtually all shops also offer advanced courses, Nitrox and night diving, and multi-dive packages, again at comparable rates. All divers also must pay US$3 per day for marine park admission and to support Cozumel's hyperbaric chambers and marine ambulance; ask if the fees are included in a shop's rates, or charged separately.

Cozumel's diver safety record is good, and there are many responsible, competent outfits in addition to those listed here. Consider this list a starting point, to be augmented by the recommendations of trusted fellow divers, travelers, locals, and expats. Most important, go with a shop you feel comfortable with, not just the cheapest, the cheeriest, or the most convenient.

Outfitters

Scuba Gamma (Calle 5 near Av. 5 Sur, tel. 987/878-4257, www.scubagamma.net, 9 A.M.–7 P.M. daily) is a mom-and-pop shop (literally) run by an amiable French family. It's one of few shops that's equipped and certified to offer diving and instruction to people with disabilities.

ScubaTony (www.scubatony.com, tel. 987/869-8628, U.S. tel. 626/593-7122) is different from most scuba operations in that it has no storefront—lower overhead typically means lower prices. American Tony Anschutz leads all

Divers relax between dives on an isolated pier in Isla Cozumel.

HOW TO CHOOSE A DIVE SHOP

There are over 100 dive shops on Isla Cozumel, and scores more at Isla Mujeres, Playa del Carmen, Cancún, Tulum, and elsewhere. Choosing just one – and then placing all your underwater faith into its hands – can be daunting. **Safety** should be your number-one concern in choosing a shop. Fortunately, the standards in Cozumel and the Riviera Maya are almost universally first rate, and accidents are rare. But that's not a reason to be complacent. For example, don't dive with a shop that doesn't ask to see your certification card or logbook – if they didn't ask you, they probably didn't ask anyone else, and an ill-trained diver is as dangerous to others in the group as he is to himself.

Equipment is another crucial issue. You should ask to inspect the shop's equipment, and the dive shop should be quick to comply. Although some casual divers are trained to evaluate gear, a good dive shop will appreciate your concern and be happy to put you at ease. If the staff is reluctant to show you the gear, either they aren't too proud of it or they don't see clients as equal partners in dive safety – both red flags.

Of course, the most important equipment is not what's on the rack but what you actually use. On the day of your dive, get to the shop early so you have time to **double-check your gear.** Old equipment is not necessarily bad equipment, but you should ask for a different BCD, wetsuit, or regulator if the condition of the one assigned to you makes you uneasy. Learn how to check the O-ring (the small rubber ring that forms the seal between the tank and the regulator) and do so before every dive. You should also attach your regulator and open the valve, to listen for any hissing between the regulator and the tank, or in the primary and backup mouthpieces. If you hear any, ask the dive master to check it and, if need be, change the regulator. Arriving early lets you do all this before getting on the boat – ideally before leaving the shop – so you can swap gear if necessary.

Feeling comfortable and free to ask questions or raise concerns (of any sort at any time) is a crucial factor in safe diving. That's where a dive shop's **personality** comes in. Every dive shop has its own culture or style, and different divers will feel more comfortable in different shops. Spend some time talking to people at a couple of different dive shops before signing up. Try to meet the person who will be leading your particular dive – you may have to come in the afternoon when that day's trip returns. Chances are one of the shops or dive masters will "click" with you.

Finally, there are some specific questions you should ask about a shop's practices. Has their air been tested and certified? Do they carry radios and oxygen? Does the captain always stay with the boat? How many people will be going on your dive? How advanced are they? And how many dive masters or instructors will there be? How experienced are they? Above all, be vocal and proactive about your safety, and remember *there are no stupid questions.*

And, of course, have fun!

his own dives and courses and offers excellent service before, during, and after your trip.

Deep Exposure Dive Center (Av. 10 Sur btwn. Calles 3 Sur and Rosado Salas, tel. 987/872-3621, toll-free U.S. tel. 866/670-2736, www.deepexposuredivecenter.com) is a small operation with friendly, professional service (and great lunches on board!).

Deep Blue (Calle Rosado Salas at Av. 10 Sur, tel. 987/872-5653, www.deepbluecozumel .com) is a long-standing shop with a reputation and track record that keep it busy even through the low season.

Liquid Blue (Av. 5 btwn. Calles Rosado Salas and 3, tel. 987/869-7794, www.liquid bluedivers.com) has somewhat higher rates than most shops, but it offers small groups and attentive, personalized service.

Careyitos Advanced Divers (Caleta harbor, near Hotel Presidente InterContinental, tel. 987/872-1578, U.S. tel. 507/434-4877, www.advanceddivers.com) caters to

DIVE INSURANCE

Although diving and snorkeling accidents are relatively rare on Cozumel, especially among beginning divers, you might consider purchasing secondary accident and/or trip insurance through the **Divers Alert Network** (DAN, toll-free U.S. tel. 800/446-2671, 24-hour emergency Mex. tel. 919/684-9111, accepts collect calls, www.diversalert network.org), a highly regarded, international, nonprofit medical organization dedicated to the health and safety of snorkelers and recreational divers. Dive accident plans cost just US$25-70 per year, including medical and decompression coverage and limited trip and lost equipment coverage. More complete trip insurance – not a bad idea in hurricane country – and life and disability coverage are also available. To be eligible for insurance, you must be a member of DAN (US$35 per year).

experienced divers, allowing up to 75 minutes bottom time and offering top-notch service.

Caribbean Divers (Av. 5 at Calle 3, tel. 987/872-1145, www.caribbeandiverscozumel .com) takes pride in its professional service and two 40-foot (12-meter) boats, which make surface intervals and getting to and from dive sites comfortable.

SNORKELING

Snorkelers have plenty of options in Cozumel, from cheap-and-easy snorkeling tours, to booking with a dive shop, to renting gear and exploring on your own, right from shore.

Most dive shops offer snorkeling as well as diving, usually visiting 2–3 sites for a half hour each (US$50–55 pp). Snorkelers often go out with a group of divers, and either snorkel in the same general location or go to a nearby site while the divers are underwater. This can mean some extra downtime as divers get in and out of the water, but the advantage is that you typically go to better and less crowded sites.

A number of shops sell snorkel tours from booths on the central passenger pier. These

trips tend to be less expensive (though with larger groups) and can be booked right as you debark from the ferry—handy if your time is short. **Cha Cha Cha Dive Shop** (Calle 7 btwn. Avs. Rafael Melgar and 5 Sur, tel. 987/872-2331, www.chachachadiveshop.com, booth opens at 8 A.M.) offers three-hour snorkeling trips on its glass-bottom boat for US$45 per person, including equipment and lunch. You'll snorkel for 30–45 minutes at each of three different sites. Its booth on the pier is easier to find than the actual shop, hidden down a narrow passage between souvenir stands and a tattoo parlor.

There are several terrific snorkeling spots near town and just offshore where you don't need a guide at all. Cozumel's boat drivers are careful about steering clear of snorkelers, but even so do not swim too far from shore, look up and around frequently, and stay out of obvious boat lanes. If you plan to do a lot of snorkeling, especially outside of established snorkeling areas, consider bringing or buying an inflatable personal buoy. Designed for snorkelers, they are brightly colored and have a string you attach to your ankle or to a small anchor weight, alerting boat drivers of your presence. Also be aware of the current, which typically runs south to north and can be quite strong.

KITEBOARDING

Kiteboarding has exploded in popularity around the world, eclipsing windsurfing among adrenaline seekers, in much the same way snowboarding has leapfrogged skiing. **Kite Cozumel** (Casa Viento, tel. 987/103-6711, www.kitecozumel.com) is the kiting outfit of Cozumel native Raul de Lille, a former Olympic-level windsurfer and now one of Mexico's top kiters and instructors. He doesn't come cheap: Private lessons are US$125/hour or US$500/day, and a three-day introductory course is US$900. For experienced kiters, de Lille offers clinics on kite control, tricks, and other specialties, plus adventuresome tours like downwinding the entire island. Kite Cozumel operates out of the hotel Casa Viento (Country Club Estates, Zona Hotelera Norte s/n, tel. 987/869-8220, www.casaviento.net), Cozumel's only kiteboarding hotel and a short walk from the island's best kiting beach.

SPORT FISHING

Cozumel boasts good deep-sea fishing year-round. It's one of few places anglers can go for the grand slam of billfishing: hooking into a blue marlin, a white marlin, a sailfish, and a swordfish all in a single day. It's also got plentiful tuna, barracuda, dorado, wahoo, grouper, and snapper.

Albatros Fishing Charters (tel. 987/872-7904, toll-free U.S. tel. 888/333-4643, www.cozumel-fishing.net) charges US$420–450 for four hours, US$500–575 for six hours, and US$575–650 for eight hours. It has a fleet of five boats, with experienced captains and crew. Boats carry a maximum of six anglers. Trips include hotel pickup and drop-off, beer and soda, snacks, bait, and gear.

Other outfits include **Wahoo Tours** (tel. 987/869-8560, toll-free U.S./Canada tel. 866/645-8977, www.wahootours.com, US$295–1,050 4–8 hrs, 4–12 people, US$150 pp shared boat up to six people) and **Go Fish** (book through www.cozumelinsider.com, US$300/4 hrs, US$350/6 hrs, up to four people).

ECOPARKS AND WATER PARKS
◖ Reserva Ecológica Faro Celarain (Punta Sur)

Once known as the Parque Ecológico Punta Sur, the Reserva Ecológica Faro Celarain (Carr. Costera Sur Km. 27, tel. 987/872-0914, www.cozumelparks.com, 9 A.M.–5 P.M. daily, US$11 adult, US$5 child over 8) spans over 1,000 hectares (2,500 acres) of coastal dunes and mangroves at the Cozumel's southern tip. Declared a national reserve in 1996, it harbors dozens of animal species, including 30 types of seabirds and a vast array of sea creatures, reptiles, and amphibians (including some huge crocs). Just past the gate, a visitors center has displays about the history and ecology of the park. A bit farther is a small Maya ruin known as El Caracol, believed to have been used for navigation; nearby there's also a high platform

overlooking Laguna Colombia for spotting birds and crocodiles. Farther still are the park's famous lighthouse and its small maritime museum. Private cars are not permitted beyond the visitors center; a park truck ferries visitors to the lighthouse as well as the beach area, where you can take a catamaran trip on the Laguna Colombia (US$3 pp, 40 mins) or just spend time sunbathing, swimming, kayaking, and snorkeling along the two kilometers (1.2 miles) of beautiful beaches. A small restaurant serves pricey food, and binoculars and snorkel gear can be rented at the visitors center if you don't have your own. Though this is a popular shore excursion for cruise-shippers, it can still be rewarding for independent travelers. Be sure to arrive before 2 P.M. if you want to take full advantage of all the park has to offer.

Parque Nacional Chankanaab

Some 9 kilometers (5.6 miles) south of town, Parque Chankanaab (Carr. Costera Sur Km. 9, tel. 987/872-0914, www.cozumelparks.com, 7 A.M.–5 P.M. daily, US$16 adult, US$8 child under 12) is a national park that doubles as a souped-up beach club. Most visitors come to spend the day sunbathing, swimming in the ocean or pool, and snorkeling. Many, however, come for the popular dolphin interaction program, run by **Dolphin Discovery** (toll-free Mex. tel. 800/727-5391, www.dolphindiscovery.com, US$78–149 adult, US$65–149 child) and offering three distinct programs that are geared to adults and children alike. It's best to reserve a spot as soon as you arrive, or better yet, book online (entry to the park is included in the price of all the dolphin programs). Park facilities include two thatch-roofed restaurants, a few gift shops, and a fully equipped dive shop. Popular with families, it is a good place to spend the day if you have little ones in tow.

GOLF

Jack Nicklaus designed the par-72 championship course at **Cozumel Country Club** (Carr. Costera Norte Km 6.5, tel. 987/872-9570, www.cozumelcountryclub.com.mx, 6:30 A.M.–6 P.M. daily), located at the far end of the northern hotel zone.

SPORT AND GAME FISHING

Cozumel and the Riviera Maya are well known for trolling and deep-sea fishing, while Ascension Bay and the Costa Maya have terrific fly-fishing. Although you can hook into just about any fish at any time of the year, the following chart lists the peak and extended seasons for a number of top target species. Those not listed – notably tuna, barracuda, yellow tail, snapper, grouper, and bonefish – are present and prevalent year-round.

SPORT FISHING

Fish	Peak Season	Extended Season
Sailfish	Mar.-June	Jan. -Sept.
Top target species, with its dramatic dorsal fin and high-flying fighting style.		
Blue Marlin	Apr.-Aug.	Mar. -Sept.
Largest Atlantic billfish, up to 500 pounds locally, but much larger elsewhere.		
White Marlin	May-July	Mar.-Aug.
Smaller than the blue marlin, but still challenging.		
Wahoo	Nov.-Jan.	June-Feb.
Lightning fast, with torpedo-like shape and distinctive blue stripes.		
Dorado	May-July	Feb.-Aug.
Hard fighter with shimmery green, gold, and blue coloration; aka dolphin or mahimahi.		

FLAT-WATER FISHING

Fish	Peak Season	Extended Season
Tarpon	Mar.-Aug.	Feb.-Oct.
Big hungry tarpon migrate along the coast in summer months.		
Snook	July-Aug.	June-Dec.
Popular trophy fish, grows locally up to 30 pounds.		
Permit	Mar.-Sept.	year-round
March and April see schools of permit, with some 20-pound individuals.		

Green fees are US$169 until 1:30 P.M., when they drop to US$105. Carts are required, and included in the rate. In addition to the slightly rolling, moderately challenging course, the club has a driving range, putting and chipping areas, overnight bag storage, a retail shop, and lessons from PGA golf pros.

For something more laid-back, **Cozumel Mini Golf** (Calle 1 at Av. 15 Sur, tel. 987/872-6570, www.czmgolf.com, 10 A.M.–11 P.M. Mon.–Sat., 5–11 P.M. Sun., US$5) features a fun and challenging 18-hole course set on a plot laden with banana trees and tropical foliage (plus a waterfall or two), just three blocks from the ferry. You'll get a walkie-talkie with your putter; use it to order $1 beers and $2 beers and sangria, delivered to you right on the green. You also can pick out a CD (from a collection of 500) to be played over the course speakers. Watch for iguanas.

SPAS AND GYMS

Acqua Spa (Carr. Costera Sur Km. 2.4, tel. 987/872-7192, www.acquaspa.com.mx, 9 A.M.–7 P.M. Mon.–Fri., until 6 P.M. Sat.) is a high-end spa offering a wide range of services including massages (US$50–125), body treatments (US$45–85), and facials (US$50–85); all spa services include 30 minutes in the steam room. The spa also offers Pilates instruction and has a gym equipped with cardio machines, weights, and more.

If you'll be in Cozumel for an extended period, **Tamart** (Calle 10 btwn. Avs. 15 and 20 Norte, 987/869-8042, www.tamart.org.mx, 7 A.M.–9 P.M. Mon.–Fri.) has yoga, salsa, jazz, and ballet instruction—among others—for adults and children. Classes typically meet three hours per week for 12 weeks and cost around US$140; the price can be pro-rated if you can't attend the full three months.

Gym Club (Av. Benito Juárez btwn. Calle 25 and Av. Pedro Joaquín Coldwell, tel. 987/872-7432, 6 A.M.–10 P.M. Mon.–Fri., 7 A.M.–5 P.M. Sat.) has free weights and weight machines in a smallish two-level exercise area. Use of the gym is US$5 a day or US$17 a week.

TOURS
Horseback Riding

Located on the inland side of the highway across from Nachi-Cocom beach club, **Rancho Palmitas** (Carr. Costera Sur Km. 16, no phone) offers two horseback tours. A 2.5-to-3-hour tour (US$40 pp) includes stops at a cavern with a cenote, the archaeological site of El Cedral, and a few unexcavated Maya ruins. A shorter 1.5-hour tour (US$30 pp) leads to the cavern only. Departures for either tour are at 8 A.M., 10 A.M., noon, 2 P.M., and 4 P.M. daily. A few additional ranches along this stretch of highway offer similar tours and rates.

Calesa Rides

Once a way for islanders to get around town, *calesas* (horse carriages) are now mainly used by tourists to see San Miguel. For US$30–35 you can hire a buggy to take you on a 30-minute tour of the town—from the waterfront to the interior. Look for the horses lined up on Avenida Rafael Melgar by Calle 1.

ATV Excursions

Though catering to cruise ship passengers, **Wild Tours** (Calle 7 btwn. Av. 5 and 10, tel. 987/872-5876, toll-free Mex. tel. 800/202-4900, www.wild-tours.com) offers ATV excursions to everyone. Tours include off-roading through the jungle, visiting isolated Maya ruins, and snorkeling at Chankanaab reef (US$75–95 adult, US$120 child with adult, 4 hours; US$60–75 adult, US$100 child with adult, 2 hours). Tours leave from a staging area in front of Carlos 'n Charlie's in Punta Langosta.

Accommodations

IN TOWN
Under US$50

One block from the central plaza, **Hostelito** (Av. 10 btwn. Av. Benito Juárez and Calle 2 Norte, tel. 987/869-8157, www.hostelcozumel.com, US$12 dorm, US$10 dorm with a/c 4 guests minimum, US$35 s/d with a/c and TV) is a stylish hostel with a spacious coed dorm with 26 orthopedic beds and fans galore. Guests are provided with clean sheets and a huge locker (BYO towel, or rent one for US$2); wireless Internet and cable TV are in the lobby. If you're traveling in a group, ask about the air-conditioned dorm with private bathroom, which is a steal at US$10 per head for up to six people. There's also a fully equipped rooftop kitchen for all to use, as well as a great lounge and solarium with hammocks for just kicking back.

Hotel Pepita (Av. 15 Sur btwn. Calles 1 and Rosado Salas, tel. 987/872-0098, US$35 s/d with a/c) is a modest but well-located and surprisingly comfortable hotel—a good value for traveler 'tweens: post-hostel but pre-B&B. The friendly owners keep the rooms very clean and well maintained. All have air-conditioning, ceiling fan, cable TV, mini-fridge, and two double beds (albeit a bit saggy). There's also fresh coffee every morning in the long inner courtyard. Same rates year-round.

Half a block from the central plaza, **Hotel Mary Carmen** (Av. 5 Sur btwn. Calles 1 and Rosado Salas, tel. 987/872-0581, www.cozumel isla.com.mx, US$40 s/d with a/c) is a simple but unexpectedly pleasant hotel. Smallish rooms have mosaic-tile headboards, good air-conditioners, and cable TV; bathrooms could stand to be remodeled but they're clean. Though not luxury, it's a good value for those on a limited budget. Ask for a room toward the back of the hotel, since the front rooms get street noise.

US$50-100

Mi Casa en Cozumel (Av. 5 btwn. Calles 7 and 9, tel. 987/872-6200, www.micasaencozumel.com, US$50–95 s/d, US$175 suite) is a terrific modern boutique hotel and an architectural gem—the curves of the spiral staircase and interior walls are counterbalanced by triangular patios and angled nooks occupied by whirlpool tubs. The hotel has nine units, each slightly different in size and layout. All have gorgeous contemporary Mexican decor, a mini-fridge, cable TV, and come with free continental breakfast served in a cozy ground-floor dining area. Two units have full kitchens and air-conditioning; the others were designed for natural ventilation and are quite comfortable with fans only. The split-level penthouse is stunning, with full kitchen, private outdoor hot tub, front and rear patios, and great views. The hotel occupies a lofty well-located structure, though it may be difficult for guests who have trouble climbing stairs.

Tamarindo Bed and Breakfast (Calle 4 btwn. Avs. 20 and 25 Norte, tel. 987/872-6190, www.tamarindocozumel.com, US$45–48 s/d with fan, US$54 s/d with a/c and mini-fridge, US$59 suite with a/c and kitchenette, US$69–79 s/d bungalow with a/c) is a pleasant bed-and-breakfast owned by a friendly French expatriate who lives on-site. The hotel has seven units bordering a large, leafy garden. Each room is different from the other, from two boxy but comfortable hotel rooms to a whimsical *palapa* bungalow with boho flair. All have cable TV and wireless Internet. A good full breakfast is included for rooms without a kitchenette; these also have access to a small communal kitchen. Rinse tanks and storage facilities are provided for guests with dive gear. Tamarindo also rents a lovely bungalow closer to the waterfront; it has two bedrooms with air-conditioning, two bathrooms, a kitchen, cable TV, and wireless Internet—perfect if you're planning to stay a while.

Amaranto Bungalows & Suites (Calle 5 btwn. Avs. 15 and 20 Sur, tel. 987/872-3219, www.tamarindoamaranto.com, US$49 s/d bungalow with a/c, US$61 s/d suite with a/c) offers seclusion and privacy, while still within easy walking distance from downtown. The shining stars of the place are the suites, in a three-story tower, each with a sitting area and 360-degree views; the lower unit has a high ceiling and modern feel, the upper one has a *palapa* roof with a lookout. There also are three thatch-roofed bungalows with modern bathrooms and attractive beachy decor. All the rooms have king-size beds, cable TV, a mini-fridge, and microwaves. Breakfast is included in all the rates. There is a plunge pool on-site—perfect for cooling off after a day in the sun. Amaranto doesn't have a full-time attendant, so it's best to call ahead to let them know when you plan to arrive.

A cozy bed-and-breakfast in the heart of San Miguel, **Villa Escondida** (Av. 10 Sur btwn. Calles 3 Sur and Rosado Salas, tel. 987/869-2203, www.cozumelvillaescondida.com, US$75–99 s/d) has just four guest rooms, each with modern comfortable beds, spacious bathrooms, and colorful decor. All look onto a sizeable interior garden with swimming pool, lounge chairs, and hammocks. A full-size breakfast—from pancakes to *chilaquiles*—is served on the hotel terrace. The place is owned and operated by a friendly Canadian-Mexican family, who live on-site and can help organize rental cars, dive trips, and more.

Vista del Mar (Av. Rafael Melgar btwn.

Calles 5 and 7 Sur, tel. 987/872-0545, toll-free U.S./Canada tel. 888/309-9988, www.hotelvista delmar.com, US$87–99 s/d with a/c) is a charming hotel in the middle of a string of tacky souvenir shops. Rooms have muted earth tones, high-end decor, inlaid stone walls, and balconies (some with spectacular views of the Caribbean). All have cable TV, mini-fridges, safety deposit boxes, robes—even turndown service. The hotel's patio also has lots of comfy lounge chairs as well as a hot tub with a mosaic-tile floor—a great space to hang if you don't mind the view of the kitsch below. A continental breakfast is included.

Suites Bahía (Calle 3 btwn. Avs. Rafael Melgar and 5 Sur, tel. 987/872-9090, toll-free Mex. tel. 800/277-2639, toll-free U.S. tel. 877/228-6747, www.suitesbahia.com, US$78–107 s/d with a/c) and **Suites Colonial** (Av. 5 Sur btwn. Calles 1 and Rosado Salas, same tel., www.suitescolonial.com, US$77 s/d with a/c, US$89 suite with a/c) are sister hotels that rent unremarkable but functional rooms and studios, most with kitchenettes. The Colonial is on the pedestrian walkway downtown and feels newer, but the rooms at the Bahía (especially the ocean-view ones) are roomier and get more natural light. Neither hotel will win any awards for charm—both look as if they've been untouched since the early 1980s—but the rooms are clean and reasonably comfortable and a kitchen can definitely be nice for longer stays. Both include air-conditioning, cable TV, continental breakfast, and wireless Internet.

Over US$100

⟨ Villas Las Anclas (Av. 5 Sur btwn. Calles 3 and 5, tel. 987/872-5476, www.lasanclas.com, US$95–125 s/d with a/c) is a great option for those who want a little home away from home. Seven pleasantly decorated apartments each have air-conditioning, a fully equipped kitchen, a living room, and a loft master bedroom up a set of spiral stairs. Using the sofas as beds, the apartments can accommodate up to four people, making a good price even better. Apartments open onto a leafy, private garden. The friendly owners live on-site and are very well informed on local dive shops, restaurants, and activities.

Casa Mexicana (Av. Rafael Melgar btwn. Calles 5 and 7, tel. 987/872-9090, toll-free Mex. tel. 800/277-2639, toll-free U.S. tel. 877/228-6747, www.casamexicanacozumel.com, US$128–162 s/d with a/c) is a modern beauty with a soaring interior courtyard and gorgeous views of the Caribbean, notwithstanding the docked cruise ships and McDonald's sign. The view is even better from the private patio of the 34 ocean-side rooms—the best are on the 5th floor. Rooms are attractive and bright, though less inspired than the building itself, with good beds, quiet air-conditioners, and updated bathrooms. There is a small infinity pool in the spacious lobby; it's a little strange to be taking a dip while watching someone check-in, but it's nice enough. Rates include a full buffet breakfast in an impressive open-air dining room. Dive packages are also available.

A long walk from town but worth every step, **⟨ Casa Colonial** (Av. 35 btwn. Calles 8 and 10, tel. 987/872-6102, toll-free U.S./Canada/Europe tel. 866/437-1320, www.cozumelrentalvillas.com, US$1,120 per week villa with a/c) has four fully equipped Mexican-style villas. All are two stories with two bedrooms, two-and-a-half bathrooms, a living room, a dining room, a modern kitchen…even a washer and dryer and wireless Internet. It's like being home with the added bonus of daily maid service. All villas face a lush courtyard with a large pool and hot tub. Dive rinse tanks are available.

Hotel Flamingo (Calle 6 btwn. Avs. Rafael Melgar and 5 Norte, tel. 987/872-1264, toll-free U.S. tel. 800/806-1601, www.hotel-flamingo.com, US$100–115 s/d, breakfast included) offers two types of rooms: The standards are just that, basic rooms with air-conditioning, cable TV, and no views; superior units offer better beds and linens, mosaic-tile bathrooms, and balconies with nice views. Ask about packages when making a reservation—there often are good deals that include diving, spa treatments, and deep-sea fishing.

OUTSIDE OF TOWN
Under US$150

Aptly named the House of Wind, **⟨ Casa**

Viento (Country Club Estates, Zona Hotelera Norte s/n, tel. 987/869-8220, www.casaviento .net, US$95–185 s/d) bills itself as a "guest house and kite camp" but appeals to kiters and non-kiters alike, with charming rooms and cheerful *"mi casa es su casa"* service from the live-in owners. Choose between large standard rooms, one- and two-bedroom suites with kitchen, and a delightful honeymoon suite with cupola and great ocean views; all rooms have air-conditioning, Wi-Fi, and deluxe linens, and most have TVs. Decor is appealingly eclectic, ranging from colonial-style arches and armoires to modern Mexican paintings and unexpected colors. A clean midsize pool and complementary snorkel gear complete the package. Casa Viento is located just minutes from some of the island's best kiteboarding spots, and is home base for Kite Cozumel, a kiting school and tour operator run by legendary Mexican kiteboarder Raul de Lille.

The only hotel on the east side of the island, **Ventanas al Mar** (south end of Playa Tortugas, no phone, www.ventanasalmar.com .mx, US$94–104 s/d, US$164–184 s/d suite) has 12 large rooms and two suites, all with high ceilings and private patios or decks, many with marvelous ocean views. The interiors lack the detailing and upkeep you'd expect at this price, but suit the hotel's isolated feel. All have kitchenettes with microwave ovens and dishes; some have mini-fridges. There's no air-conditioning, as the hotel runs almost entirely on wind and solar power. Fortunately, the constant sea breeze keeps rooms cool. There's a good restaurant next door, but you'll probably want a car, as the east side has no ATM, grocery stores, or other services. Or you can embrace the isolation: Many guests spend a week or more without going to town at all. Rates include a full breakfast.

It should come as no surprise that the **Fiesta Americana Cozumel Dive Resort** (Carr. Sur Km. 7.5, tel. 987/872-9600, toll-free U.S. tel. 800/343-7821, www.fiestamericana.com, US$108–143 s/d with a/c, US$202–221 suite with a/c) caters to divers. Most people who stay here spend their days (and part of their nights) underwater and use the resort's well-regarded dive shop. The hotel itself is comfortable,

though rooms vary significantly in style: Ask for one of the refurbished ones, which are sleek and modern, with marble floors and dark wood furnishings. There is also a well-tended pool and a small artificial beach that has barriers to hold in the imported sand—not what you'd expect when you think Caribbean beach, but nice enough if you just want to take in the sun.

Over US$150

An easy 15-minute walk north of town is **Condumel Condominiums** (Zona Hotelera Norte Km. 1.5, tel. 987/872-0892, www.condumel.com, US$159 apartment with a/c), an old school but well-kept condominium complex on the main road. Each of the 10 one-bedroom apartments is spacious and has air-conditioning, a king-size bed, a marble bathroom, and a fully equipped kitchen—the refrigerator even comes stocked with basics so that you don't have to go grocery shopping right away. Oversized sliding-glass doors offer views of the Caribbean—which is spectacular at sunset—and incoming airplanes. The coast here is iron shore, so it's rocky, but a small semi-protected cove with steps and a ladder is perfect for swimming and snorkeling; there's even a diving board that screams cannonball. A small sandy area with lounge chairs also has been set up for guests who need a daily beach fix. Wireless Internet is available.

(Presidente InterContinental Cozumel Resort Spa (Carr. Sur Km. 6.5, tel. 987/872-9500, toll-free Mex. tel. 800/000-6633, toll-free U.S. tel. 888/424-6835, www.intercontinental.com, US$440 s/d with a/c, US$952 suite with a/c) may well be the best hotel-resort in Cozumel with spacious, classy rooms featuring flat-screen TVs, stereos, and turndown service. While the views are of either garden or ocean, all roads lead to one of the best hotel beaches on the island—thick white sand and calm, turquoise waters with excellent access for snorkelers and shore divers. A well-regarded dive shop, two lighted tennis courts, three restaurants, a pool, and a full-service spa round out an already relaxing stay.

North of town and near the country club, **Playa Azul Hotel** (Zona Hotelera Norte Km.

4, tel. 987/869-5160, www.playa-azul.com, US$246–340 s/d) caters mostly to golfers, but it has packages for divers and honeymooners as well. Even if you don't golf much, you may as well get in a round or two if you stay here— guests pay no green fees. Medium-size rooms have modern furnishings and large bathrooms; most have a terrace with chairs and excellent ocean views. Top-floor rooms have a little cupola on the bedroom, a nice touch. The pool is clean and attractive, but the beach (already small) can get crowded with day guests visiting the hotel's beach club. That said, the overall atmosphere here is calm and quiet, removed from the noise and activity downtown.

The all-inclusive **Iberostar Cozumel** (Carr. Sur Km. 17.8, tel. 987/872-9900, toll-free U.S./Canada tel. 888/923-2722, US$290/500 s/d) is a favorite among repeat visitors to the island. It's a mellow place with simple but comfortable rooms set up in two-story bungalows around the verdant property. There are two à la carte restaurants—Mexican cuisine and a steak house— plus a buffet, snack bar, and room service. Like most all-inclusives, there's nightly entertainment, which is hit or miss—just go with it—and daily activities like water aerobics and yoga. It also has a wide sandy beach, though the entry into the water can be a bit rocky—be sure to bring water shoes. All in all, the place offers great value.

Food

Cozumel isn't known as a culinary hot spot, but you do have plenty of options. Like any island it has terrific seafood (though many people are surprised to learn that much of the catch actually comes from around Isla Mujeres because the waters around Cozumel are protected areas). And the island's popularity with Americans, especially hungry Texan divers, means you'll never want for a steak, pasta, fajitas, or a big breakfast.

MEXICAN AND YUCATECAN

Sabores (Av. 5 btwn. Calles 3 and 5, noon–4 P.M. Mon.–Fri., US$5–13) is a family-run restaurant operated out of a bright yellow house. A wide variety of traditional Mexican dishes are served as *comidas corridas* with soup, main dish, and fruit drink running US$4–8. Clients can choose between eating in the converted living room or under the shade trees in the backyard. Check out the dry-erase board for the daily offerings.

The breezy *palapa*-roofed **La Candela** (Av. 5 at Calle 6 Norte, tel. 987/878-4471, 8 A.M.–6 P.M. Mon.–Sat., US$3–9) is a favorite among locals and expats. Every day, a lineup of Mexican and traditional Yucatecan dishes is offered in a cafeteria-style setting. Check out

what's steaming behind the glass window cases, find a seat, then place your order with your waiter. Lunch specials typically include soup or pasta, a main dish, and a drink.

Set in an old yellow clapboard house, **Casa Denis** (Calle 1 btwn. Avs. 5 and 10 Sur, tel. 987/872-0067, 7 A.M.–11 P.M. Mon.–Sat., 6–11 P.M. Sun., US$5–15) serves up reliable Mexican and Yucatecan meals every day of the week. Most tables are outdoors and face the pedestrian walkway, making it a great spot for people-watching. It's made even better with a cold beer and fresh fish empanadas, one of the restaurant's tastiest dishes.

From the moment it opens, the high thatched roof at **La Choza** (Av. 10 at Calle Rosado Salas, tel. 987/872-0958, 7 A.M.–10:30 P.M., US$6–19) is aswirl with the rich smell and sound of traditional Mexican and Tex-Mex cuisine: Almost everything on the menu involves some sort of sizzling meat. Some dishes are great, others miss badly, but that doesn't prevent loyal patrons from packing the place most days. Service is fast and friendly.

Pancho's Backyard (Av. Rafael Melgar 27 btwn. Avs. 8 and 10 Norte, tel. 987/872-2141, 10 A.M.–11 P.M. Mon.–Sat., 5–11 P.M. Sun., US$11–24) is Mexico epitomized—gurgling fountains, colonial-style decor, and marimba music. Add creative haute cuisine such as chiles rellenos (peppers stuffed with bananas and walnut) and *camarones a la naranja* (orange shrimp flambéed in tequila) and you'll leave wanting to return. Popular with cruise ship travelers, the restaurant is big enough that it never feels crowded.

SEAFOOD

El Capi Navegante (Av. 10 Sur btwn. Calles 3 and 5, tel. 987/872-1730, 7 A.M.–10 P.M. daily, US$15–30) is a nautical-themed favorite on the island, serving some of the freshest seafood around (and well-priced breakfasts, too). Try the *Parrillada El Capi*—an enormous dish of grilled fish, shrimp, octopus, conch, and squid. There are mariachi performances most nights.

Bahía del Caribe (Av. 5 Sur btwn. Calles 9 and 9-bis, noon–8 P.M. daily US$5–15) is a low-key eatery run by a local fishermen's cooperative, so the fish is especially fresh and well-priced. Whole fried fish is US$9 per kilo, and even a half kilo makes for a hefty meal; there are also a dozen different ceviche and cocktail options, and just as many fillets. Eat in the large yet simple semi-outdoor dining area, or order to go if it's near closing time.

A family-run restaurant, **❰ La Conchita del Caribe** (Av. 65 btwn. Calles 13 and 15, tel. 987/872-5888, 11:30 A.M.–7:30 P.M. daily, US$9–16) is another local favorite. The seafood is super fresh—just about anything you choose was swimming that day. If ordering a whole fish, pick it out of a cooler by the counter (and be sure to tell your waiter whether or not you want the head left on). Takeout is also available.

Specializing in northern Italian seafood dishes, **Prima Trattoria** (Calle Rosado Salas at Av. 5, tel. 987/872-4242, 4–11 P.M. daily, US$8–25) serves up homemade pastas and great salads too. If you can't decide what to order, try the seafood linguine, a hearty dish that's especially tasty. Seating is on a charming rooftop garden—perfect on a warm night. Reservations are recommended.

OTHER SPECIALTIES

With a shady courtyard and a seemingly endless list of sauces, **❰ Guido's** (Av. Rafael Melgar btwn. Calles 6 and 8, tel. 987/872-0946, 11 A.M.–11 P.M. Mon.–Sat., US$8–17) is perfect if you're in the mood for a special pasta dish or brick-oven pizza. Add a glass of sangria and a warm breeze and you've got the makings for the ultimate Cozumeleño night out. The place is popular with expatriates and locals.

Considered one of the best restaurants in town, **❰ La Cocay** (Calle 8 btwn. Avs. 10 and 15, tel. 987/872-5533, 5–11 P.M. Mon.–Sat., US$9–30) offers Mediterranean cuisine with flair. The menu changes seasonally but expect to see dishes like sautéed scallops with cognac glaze, and blue cheese–filled phyllo dough rolls with black cherry sauce. Seating is in a candlelit dining room or on the breezy garden patio. It's perfect for a special night out.

With waterfront views, **Chi** (above Pizza Hut, Calle 3 at Av. Rafael Melgar, tel. 987/869-8156, www.chicozumel.com, 9:30 A.M.–midnight Mon.–Wed., 9:30 A.M.–2 A.M. Thurs.–Sat., noon–midnight Sun., US$8–15) offers an extensive Asian menu of over 200 items in a pleasant setting. Chinese, Thai, Japanese, and Filipino dishes figure prominently but the chefs prepare food to order—just let them know what you're craving.

Especias (Calle 3 near Av. 5 Sur, tel. 987/876-1558, 5–11 P.M. Mon.–Sat., US$5–10) is a small restaurant serving a large variety of cuisines—Argentinean, Jamaican, Thai, Indian, and more. The zucchini stuffed with cheese and tomatoes and the *chistorro* (rolled thin sausage) are especially good ways to start your meal.

Pepe's Grill (Av. Rafael Melgar btwn. Calles Rosado Salas and 3, tel. 987/872-0213, 5–11 P.M. daily, US$12–24) has long been popular for its good food and sunset views over the Caribbean. It's definitely old school, harkening back to the mid-1980s in its nautical style and synthesizer jam sessions, but if you're in the mood for prime rib or a big salad, this is the place to come.

Jeanie's Beach Club (Av. Rafael Melgar near Calle 11, tel. 987/878-4647, 6 A.M.–11 P.M. daily, US$6–15) offers a wide variety of dishes, but the main reason to eat here are the made-to-order waffles served in every shape, way, and form—they even replace tortillas as the base for traditional *huevos rancheros*. Portions are hearty so come hungry.

The world's smallest **Hard Rock Café** (Av. Rafael Melgar near Av. Benito Juárez, tel. 987/878-4268, 10 A.M.–1 A.M. Sun.–Wed., 10 A.M.–2 A.M. Thurs.–Sat., US$6–18) has views of the Caribbean during the day and live music starting at 10 P.M. Thursday–Saturday. Food is typical Hard Rock fare (i.e., stick to the burgers) and a boutique near the entrance sells T-shirts and rock 'n' roll memorabilia.

CAFÉS AND BISTROS

With a tree growing through the middle of the main dining area and regular art exhibits on the walls, **◖ Coffeelia** (Calle 5 btwn. Avs. 5 Sur and Rafael Melgar, tel. 987/872-7402, 7:30 A.M.–11 P.M. Mon.–Sat., 9 A.M.–2 P.M. and 5–10 P.M. Sun., US$4–7) is a pleasing, bohemian place. The food, too, is a pleasure—light and varied with a dozen egg dishes, 18 crepe combos, and a small army of sandwiches and salads. It's a great place to kick back with a café au lait and catch up on postcards.

Restaurante del Museo (Av. Rafael Melgar and Calle 6, tel. 987/872-0838, 7 A.M.–2 P.M. daily, US$4–7) is a little outdoor café on the roof of the Museo Cozumel, great for lunch after a morning at the museum or simply for a drink to watch the boats cruise past. Get there early on Sundays, when locals line up for the restaurant's famous *sopa de pancita* (cow's stomach soup)—an acquired, kind of furry taste.

A tiny bistro on a quiet corner, **Le Chef** (Av. 5 at Calle 5 Sur, tel. 987/878-4391, 2–11 P.M. Mon.–Sat., 6–11 P.M. Sun., US$7–20) serves

up gourmet kosher meals and sandwiches, fancy cheese plates, gourmet pizza and pasta, and big salads. Service is molasses slow, but the electic decor, mellow tunes, and a glass of wine (or two) helps the time pass a little faster.

If you notice the aroma of roasting beans, follow your nose to **Café Chiapas** (Calle 2 btwn. Avs. 5 and 10 Norte, tel. 987/869-2042, 8 A.M.–8 P.M. Mon.–Fri., until 2 P.M. Sat.). This place sells some of the best coffee around, though with just one stool and a countertop, you'll have to take it to go.

SWEETS

Hands down, the best place to go for traditional Mexican baked goods is **Zermatt** (Av. 5 Norte at Calle 4, tel. 987/872-1384, 7 A.M.–8:30 P.M. Mon.–Sat., 7 A.M.–6 P.M. Sun.).

If the bread is still baking at Zermatt, try **Panadería Cozumeleña** (Av. 10 Sur at Calle 3, 7 A.M.–10 P.M. Mon.–Sat., 7 A.M.–9 P.M. Sun.) for a good sampling of Mexican breads and pastries.

For a cool treat, head to **La Flor de Michoacán** (Calle 1 near Av. 10, 9 A.M.–11 P.M. daily), where there's always a variety of homemade *aguas* (fruit drinks), *nieves* (ice cream), and *paletas* (popsicles).

GROCERIES

If you are cooking for yourself, **Chedraui** (Av. Rafael Melgar btwn. Calles 15 and 17, 7 A.M.–10 P.M. daily) is the largest supermarket on the island.

For a traditional market experience—fresh produce and sides of beef hanging from hooks—head to the **Mercado Municipal** (Av. 25 btwn. Calles 1 and Rosado Salas, 7 A.M.–3 P.M. daily).

Information and Services

TOURIST INFORMATION

The city tourist office has three **information booths** (8 A.M.–7 P.M. Mon.–Sat., 9 A.M.–2 P.M. Sun.)—in the central plaza, at the international pier, and at Puerta Maya pier. The only distinguishing feature between the tourist information booths and tour operators' kiosks is that staffers don't push area trips. English is spoken at all locations.

The *Free Blue Guide to Cozumel* has good maps and listings for a range of services, from restaurants to dive shops. Look for the booklet as you get off the ferry.

The website www.thisiscozumel.com is an excellent all-around resource, combining up-to-date tourist information with suggested outings and light reporting on important island issues.

EMERGENCY SERVICES

Centro Médico de Cozumel (CMC, Calle 1A Sur at Av. 50, tel. 987/872-9400, www.centromedicodecozumel.com.mx, 24 hours) accepts many foreign insurance plans, though the prices tend to be high. A good alternative is the **Clínica-Hospital San Miguel** (Calle 6 Norte btwn. Avs. 5 and 10, tel. 987/872-0103, 24 hours), offering general medical services. Cozumel's **Hyperbaric Medical Center** (Calle 5 btwn. Avs. Rafael Melgar and 5 Sur, tel. 987/872-1430, 7 A.M.–10 P.M. daily, on-call 24 hours) specializes in diver-related medical treatment, though non-diving ailments are also treated. For meds, try **Farmacia Similares** (Calle 1 Sur at Av. 15 Norte, tel. 987/869-2440, 24 hours).

The **tourist police** (Calle 11 Sur near Av. Rafael Melgar, 8 A.M.–11 P.M. daily) are stationed in a kiosk near Punta Langosta, though officers can often be found patrolling the central plaza. The **police station** (Palacio Municipal, Calle 13 btwn. Avs. 5 and Rafael Melgar, tel. 987/872-0092, 24 hours) can be reached toll-free at 066.

MONEY

Accessing your money is not difficult in Cozumel, especially near the central plaza.

HSBC (Av. 5 Sur at Calle 1, 8 A.M.–7 P.M. Mon.–Sat.), **Bancomer** (Av. 5 Sur btwn. Av. Juárez and Calle 1, 8:30 A.M.–4 P.M. Mon.–Fri.), and **Banorte** (Av. 5 Norte btwn. Av. Juárez and Calle 2, 9 A.M.–5 P.M. Mon.–Fri., 9 A.M.–2 P.M. Sat.) all have ATMs and exchange foreign cash.

MEDIA AND COMMUNICATIONS

Cozumel's **post office** (Av. Rafael Melgar at Calle 7, 9 A.M.–5 P.M. Mon.–Fri., 9 A.M.–1 P.M. Sat.) is next to Punta Langosta shopping center.

There are myriad Internet cafes where you can get online, make international phone calls, burn photos to CDs, and more. **Blau Net** (Calle Rosado Salas btwn. Avs. 10 and 15, tel. 987/872-6275, 9 A.M.–10 P.M. Mon.–Sat.) is a quiet reliable place charging US$1 per hour of Internet use and US$0.40 per minute for calls to the United States and Canada. **Web Station** (Av. 5 Sur btwn. Calles 3 and 5, tel. 987/872-3911, 9 A.M.–11 P.M. Mon.–Sat., 10 A.M.–10 P.M. Sun.) charges the same rates and has wicked air-conditioning.

IMMIGRATION AND CONSULATES

The immigration office (Av. 15 Sur at Calle 5, tel. 987/872-3110) is open 9 A.M.–1 P.M. Monday–Friday; there's also an office at the airport (tel. 987/872-5604, 7 A.M.–9 P.M. daily).

The **U.S. Consular Agency** (Plaza Villamar, central plaza, tel. 987/872-4574, usgov@cozumel.net) is open noon–2 P.M. Monday–Friday.

LAUNDRY

Lavandería Margarita (Av. 20 btwn. Av. 3 and Calle Rosado Salas, no phone, 7 A.M.–9 P.M. Mon.–Sat., 8 A.M.–5 P.M. Sun.) charges US$2.50 per load plus US$1.50 every 10 minutes in the dryer—it's not cheap, but options are limited on the island.

Getting There and Around

GETTING THERE

Air

Cozumel International Airport (CZM, tel. 987/872-0485) is approximately three kilometers (2 miles) from downtown. The airport has an ATM in the departures area, AmEx currency exchange at arrivals, and a few magazine stands and duty-free shops. Private taxis from the airport run US$11–38, depending on the distance to your hotel, while shared taxis are US$5–11 per person, departing every 5–30 minutes. (You also can save money by booking round-trip service.)

Bus

Although there are no long-distance buses on Cozumel (it is a pretty small island, after all), you can buy tickets for buses departing from Playa del Carmen at **Ticket Bus** (main ferry pier, Av. Rafael Melgar, no phone, 6:30 A.M.–1:30 P.M. and 2–9 P.M. daily); there's a second office at the corner of Calle 2 and Avenida 10 Sur (tel. 987/869-2553, 6 A.M.–2 P.M. and 2:30–9 P.M. daily). There is a US$0.70 surcharge for all tickets, but it's a small price to pay to be sure you'll have a spot once you get to Playa.

Ferry

Ferries to Playa del Carmen (US$11 each way, 30 mins) leave from the passenger ferry pier across from the central plaza. Two companies—**UltraMar** (Av. Rosado Salas at Av. 45, tel. 987/869-3223) and **Mexico Waterjets** (Calle 6 Norte btwn. Avs. 20 and 25, tel. 987/872-1578)—operate the boats; the service and fares are identical, though UltraMar's boats are somewhat newer. Between the two companies, at least one ferry leaves Cozumel every hour on the hour from 5 A.M. to 10 P.M. daily.

Car ferries operated by **Transcaribe** (tel. 987/872-7688) depart from Cozumel's international pier at 6 A.M., 11 A.M., 4 P.M., and 8:30 P.M. Monday to Saturday and at 8 A.M. and 8 P.M. on Sunday. On the mainland, the ferries come and go from the Calica/Punta Venado dock south of Playa del Carmen at 1:30 P.M. and 6 P.M. Monday to Saturday (earlier departures are for freight only) and at 6 A.M. and 6 P.M. on Sunday. The trip takes about 1.25 hours and costs US$45 for a car including driver, and US$5 for each additional passenger. Arrive at least an hour in advance, each way, to get a spot.

FLYING TO COZUMEL

The following airlines service Cozumel International Airport (CZM):

- **AeroCozumel** (airport tel. 987/872-0468)

- **Aeroméxico** (airport tel. 987/872-3454, toll-free Mex. tel. 800/021-4010, www.aeromexico.com)

- **American Airlines** (toll-free Mex. tel. 800/904-6000, toll-free U.S. tel. 800/433-7300, www.aa.com)

- **Click Mexicana** (airport tel. 987/872-3456, toll-free Mex. tel. 800/112-5425, www.clickmx.com)

- **Continental** (airport tel. 987/872-0847, toll-free Mex. tel. 800/900-5000, toll-free U.S. tel. 800/523-3273, www.continental.com)

- **Delta** (toll-free Mex. tel. 800/123-4710, toll-free U.S. tel. 800/221-1212, www.delta.com)

- **Mexicana** (airport tel. 987/872-2945, toll-free Mex. tel. 800/502-2000, www.mexicana.com)

- **US Airways** (toll-free U.S. tel. 800/428-4322, www.usairways.com)

© LIZA PRADO

The passenger ferries from Playa del Carmen arrive in front of Cozumel's central plaza.

GETTING AROUND

In town, you can easily walk anywhere you like. However, the powerful taxi union has succeeded in quashing any and all efforts to start public bus service out of town and around the island. It is a shame, really, since it would be so easy and convenient to have a fleet of buses making loops around the island, or even just up and down the western shore. Until that changes (don't hold your breath), you'll need a car, moped, or bike to explore the rest of the island.

Bicycle

A bike can be handy for getting to beach clubs and snorkel sites outside of town. Traffic on Avenida Rafael Melgar can be heavy south of town, but once clear of that, the roadway is relatively unhurried. **Rentadora Gallo** (Av. 10 Sur btwn. Calle 1 and Av. Benito Juárez, tel. 987/869-2444, 8 A.M.–7 P.M. daily) rents bicycles for around US$15 per day, as well as snorkel gear (US$15 per day).

Taxi

Taxis (tel. 987/872-0236 or 987/872-0041) are everywhere—you can easily flag one down on Avenida Rafael Melgar, near the main passenger pier, and around the plaza. Cabs typically charge US$1.50–3 around town, US$3.50 from the center to the airport, and US$7 for a hotel pick-up. For hotels and beach clubs out of town, the rates jump significantly, from US$7 to as much as US$40 for Punta Sur. As always, agree on a price before getting into a taxi.

Car and Moped Rental

Renting a car is a nice way to get out of downtown and see the rest of the island. It is virtually impossible to get lost, and you can visit all the main spots in a day or two.

If you do decide to rent some wheels, go to the agency yourself—do not allow one of the friendly guys at the pier to lead you there. They are *comisionistas,* freelancers who earn hefty commissions for bringing tourists to particular shops, which then pass the cost on to you. Shop owners go along begrudgingly; if they decline the "service," the same freelancers will actively steer future tourists away from the shop, saying it's closed, burned down, fresh out of cars— you get the idea.

ISLA COZUMEL

Taxi drivers wait in a long line for arriving cruise ship passengers.

Excluding commissions, rental cars in Cozumel start at US$35–50 a day for a VW bug or other small car, including insurance and taxes. Mopeds rent for around US$20 a day. Be aware that scooters account for the majority of accidents here, as speed bumps, potholes, and windy conditions can upend even experienced drivers. Also remember that unpaved roads are not covered by most rental car insurance plans.

Rentadora Isis (Av. 5 Norte btwn. Calles 2 and 4, tel. 987/872-3367, rentadoraisis@prodigy.net.mx, 8 A.M.–6:30 P.M. Mon.–Sat., 8 A.M.–6 P.M. Sun.) consistently has the island's best rates, and friendly service to boot.

Rentadora Gallo (Av. 10 Sur btwn. Calle 1 and Av. Benito Juárez, tel. 987/869-2444, 8 A.M.–7 P.M. daily) is also eager to please. **Budget** (Av. 5 Norte btwn. Calles 2 and 4, tel. 987/872-0903, www.budgetcancun.com, 7 A.M.–7 P.M. daily) is one of a handful of international companies on the island. **Hertz** and **Avis** have booths at the airport.

Cozumel has three PEMEX gas stations (7 A.M.–midnight daily). Two are in town on Avenida Benito Juárez (at Avs. Pedro Joaquin Coldwell and 75) and the third is four kilometers (2.5 miles) south of town on the Carretera Costera Sur across from Puerta Maya, the main cruise ship pier.

THE RIVIERA MAYA

Cancún may be the name everyone recognizes, but for many people—especially repeat visitors—the best of Mexico's Caribbean coast is the Riviera Maya. Stretching more than 130 kilometers (80 miles) south from Cancún to Tulum, the Riviera Maya is home to fast-growing cities like Playa del Carmen, low-key towns like Puerto Morelos, and tiny beachfront settlements like Tankah Tres. It boasts megaresorts and tiny bed-and-breakfasts and is flanked by the world's longest underground river on one side of the coastal highway and the world's second-longest coral reef on the other. While recent hurricanes have sucked away much of Cancún's famous talcum-power sand, a whole lot of it has washed ashore along the Riviera Maya, where the beaches are as wide and glorious as ever.

There's plenty to see and do, much of it do-it-yourself: go snorkeling in freshwater cenotes and lagoons, help release newly hatched sea turtles into the sea, explore little-visited Maya ruins, or spend the day at a family-friendly ecopark. For party-hounds, Cancún still has a lock on over-the-top nightspots, but there are plenty of places to cut loose in the Riviera Maya, especially lounge bars, beach parties, and resort nightclubs. (Besides, you can always hop a shuttle to Cancún or join a club crawl if you really need a Coco Bongo fix.)

With so many options, the main trouble here may be fitting it all in. Then again, when you're vacationing in a place as beautiful as the Riviera Maya, doing nothing may well be the highlight of your trip!

© LIZA PRADO

THE RIVIERA MAYA

HIGHLIGHTS

◖ Puerto Morelos's Coral Reef: Skip the tourist-trap snorkeling trips in Cancún and Playa del Carmen and go snorkeling where the reef is still healthy, the water uncrowded, and the price unbeatable. Book a tour with a local dive shop or the long-operating fishermen's cooperative (page 41).

◖ Playa del Carmen's Quinta Avenida: Ever-growing yet wonderfully walkable, Playa's 5th Avenue has block after block of tempting restaurants, hipster boutiques, and lively bars. The ferry and bus terminals are at the busy southern end, while the northern end is cooler and quieter, with a distinctive European flair (page 50).

◖ Playa del Carmen's Beaches and Beach Clubs: Playa's beaches are already among the Riviera Maya's most beautiful, and its beach clubs — with lounge chairs and beach beds for rent, wait service on the sand, lockers and changing rooms, even swimming pools and the occasional DJ — make them some of the most enjoyable, too (page 51).

◖ Xcaret Ecopark: The Riviera Maya's elaborate ecoparks are a hit with parents looking for a safe, active, friendly place to take the kids. Xcaret is the most ambitious of them all, with tubing and snorkeling, an aquarium and animal enclosures, orchid greenhouse, and an end-of-the-day extravaganza performance (page 51).

◖ Laguna Yal-Ku: A long elbow of water fed by freshwater cenotes and draining into the ocean, this Akumal-area lagoon is a favorite among snorkelers for its colorful fish and jumble of underwater rocks and channels.

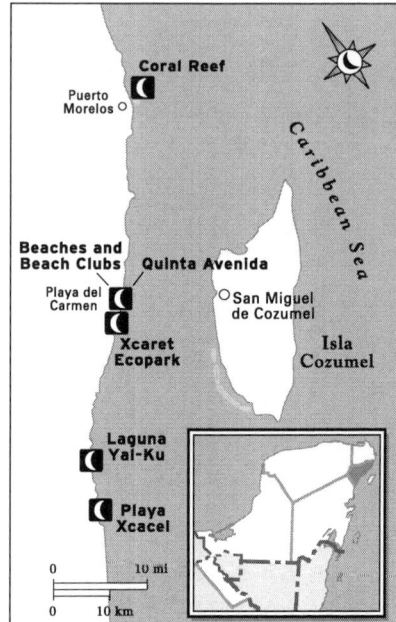

LOOK FOR **◖** TO FIND RECOMMENDED SIGHTS, ACTIVITIES, DINING, AND LODGING.

Parking and a changing area make it an easy and accessible stop (page 78).

◖ Playa Xcacel: Just off the highway down an easy-to-miss sand road, this glorious stretch of white-sand beach has nary a beach bed or banana boat in sight. The secret? It's a major sea-turtle nesting area, and protected from development — at least for now (page 85).

PLANNING YOUR TIME

You'll probably want to pick a home base (or two) for your time here, and make day trips from there. Playa del Carmen is the area's only real city, with all the expected urban amenities, including nightlife. (It's also the gateway to Isla Cozumel.) Puerto Morelos and Akumal are smaller, but still have a decent selection of hotels and restaurants. (In fact, if you're a foodie, Puerto Morelos has a surprising number of first-rate restaurants.) If isolation is more important than convenience, the Riviera Maya has some secret getaways, like Xpu-Há

and Tankah Tres. If you've got a week or more, consider spending half your time in the northern section—around Playa del Carmen, for example—and then move farther south, to enjoy Akumal, Tankah Tres, and even Tulum.

A rental car isn't absolutely necessary, but will certainly make exploring the Riviera Maya a lot easier. Cheap public shuttles zip up and down the coast, but they only stop along the highway, which in most places is about a kilometer from the ocean. That leaves you to make the hot dusty walk up and down the access roads, especially in more rural areas where taxis are uncommon.

Puerto Morelos

Somehow little Puerto Morelos has escaped the mega-development that has swept up and down the Riviera Maya, despite being squeezed between the booming cities of Cancún and Playa del Carmen. It remains, for the most part, a quiet seaside town. Yes, the town fills up with foreign tourists in the high season—and more and more condos and resorts are cropping up—but it is still a place where a substantial part of the local population lives by fishing, where life revolves around the central plaza, and where kids and dogs romp in the streets.

Local residents fought tirelessly and ultimately succeeded in having the portion of reef and shoreline in front of Puerto Morelos designated a national reserve. So while the beach isn't great, the snorkeling and diving are, and a town cooperative and local dive shops run recommended and affordable tours. Puerto Morelos is also gaining popularity as a destination for yoga and meditation groups—no surprise given its serene atmosphere—and a growing number of hotels and resorts cater to that market.

Be aware that the low season here is *very* low and many businesses close in May, September, and/or October.

SIGHTS
Playa Principal
The main beach at Puerto Morelos is

disappointing—rocky in many places and elsewhere strewn with seaweed that has washed ashore. The best spot is at the Ojo de Agua hotel (Av. Javier Rojo Gómez near Ejército Mexicano), which rents beach chairs to nonguests for US$2.50 apiece, or fixed *palapa* umbrellas (US$10/15 medium/large) with four beach chairs and a small table—a good option for families. There's a serviceable restaurant, and you can use the hotel's swimming pool as well.

Coral Reef
Puerto Morelos's most spectacular attraction is snorkeling on the reef. Directly in front of the village, around 500 meters (0.3 mile) offshore, the reef here takes on gargantuan dimensions—up to 30 meters (99 feet) wide. Winding passages and large caverns alive with fish and sea flora make for great exploring. And since it's a marine reserve and fishing and motor traffic are limited, the reef is more pristine here than almost any place along the Riviera. A **local cooperative** (8 A.M.–3 P.M. Mon.–Sat., US$25 pp for 1.5 hrs) offers tours of the reef, with boats leaving every 30 minutes from the municipal pier.

The Central Plaza
Puerto Morelos's peaceful central plaza has always been a highlight of the town, but a recent

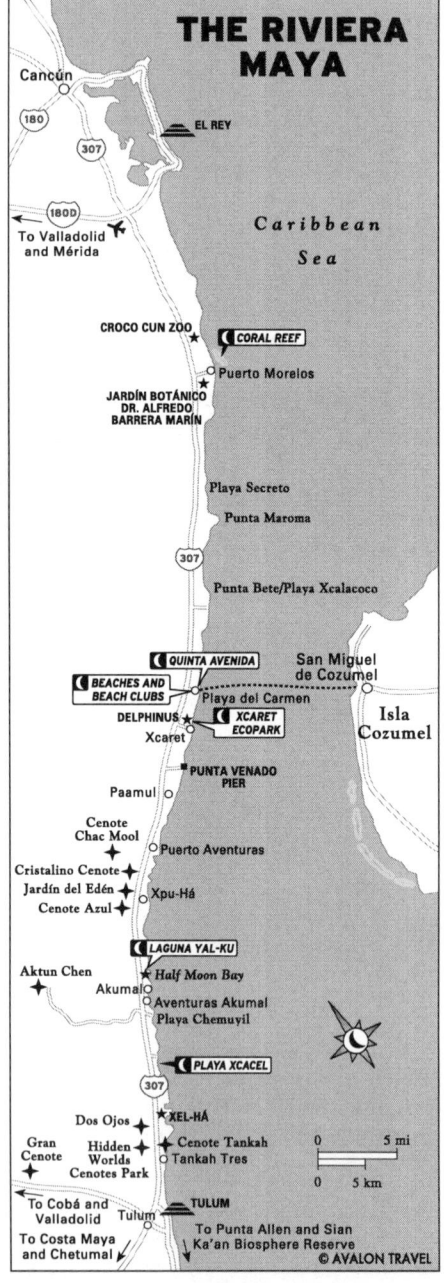

THE RIVIERA MAYA

To Valladolid and Mérida

Caribbean Sea

Cancún

EL REY

To Valladolid and Mérida

CROCO CUN ZOO

CORAL REEF

Puerto Morelos

JARDÍN BOTÁNICO DR. ALFREDO BARRERA MARÍN

Playa Secreto

Punta Maroma

Punta Bete/Playa Xcalacoco

QUINTA AVENIDA

BEACHES AND BEACH CLUBS

Playa del Carmen

DELPHINUS

XCARET ECOPARK

Xcaret

San Miguel de Cozumel

Isla Cozumel

PUNTA VENADO PIER

Paamul

Cenote Chac Mool

Cristalino Cenote

Jardín del Edén

Cenote Azul

Puerto Aventuras

Xpu-Há

LAGUNA YAL-KU

Aktun Chen

Half Moon Bay

Akumal

Aventuras Akumal

Playa Chemuyil

PLAYA XCACEL

Dos Ojos

Gran Cenote

Hidden Worlds

Cenotes Park

XEL-HÁ

Cenote Tankah

Tankah Tres

To Cobá and Valladolid

Tulum

TULUM

To Costa Maya and Chetumal

To Punta Allen and Sian Ka'an Biosphere Reserve

0   5 mi

0   5 km

© AVALON TRAVEL

facelift has made it even more appealing. New paint, better landscaping, and an improved play structure for kids make it a great place to while away the early evening hours, especially for families. Locals and visitors alike mingle on shaded benches and in the bleachers facing the basketball court (whose baskets cleverly double as soccer goal posts). Many of Puerto Morelos' best restaurants face the plaza, or are just a block away, so you're sure to pass by more than once. On Sundays, a small *tianguis* (flea market) is held here, and you can have fun browsing through someone else's old treasures.

Croco Cun Zoo

This charming little tropical petting zoo (tel. 998/850-3719, www.crococunzoo.com, 9 A.M.–6 P.M. daily, US$19 adult, US$12 child 6–12, free under 6) is located five kilometers (3.1 miles) north of the Puerto Morelos turnoff. Ninety-minute guided tours, offered in English or Spanish, bring visitors up close and personal to all sorts of local creatures—if you're up for it, you can feed spider monkeys on your shoulder, walk through a crocodile enclosure, and hold boas, iguanas, and baby crocs. Don't forget your camera. Well-managed and reasonably affordable—compare this to swimming with the dolphins!—Croco Cun is a sure hit for youngsters and adults alike.

Jardín Botánico Dr. Alfredo Barrera Marín

A half kilometer (0.75 mile) south of the Puerto Morelos turnoff is a peaceful botanical garden (tel. 983/835-0440, 8 A.M.–4 P.M. daily Nov.–Apr., 9 A.M.–5 P.M. daily May–Oct., US$7), study center, and tree nursery spread over 60 hectares (150 acres). Two kilometers (1.2 miles) of trails wind beneath a canopy of trees and past many of the peninsula's plants and flowers, each with its name labeled in English, Spanish, and Latin. Habitats vary from semi-evergreen tropical forest to mangrove swamp. Look for the epiphyte area, with a variety of orchids, tillandsias, and bromeliads. As you wander around you'll also find a re-creation of a Maya *chiclero* camp (showing how chicle

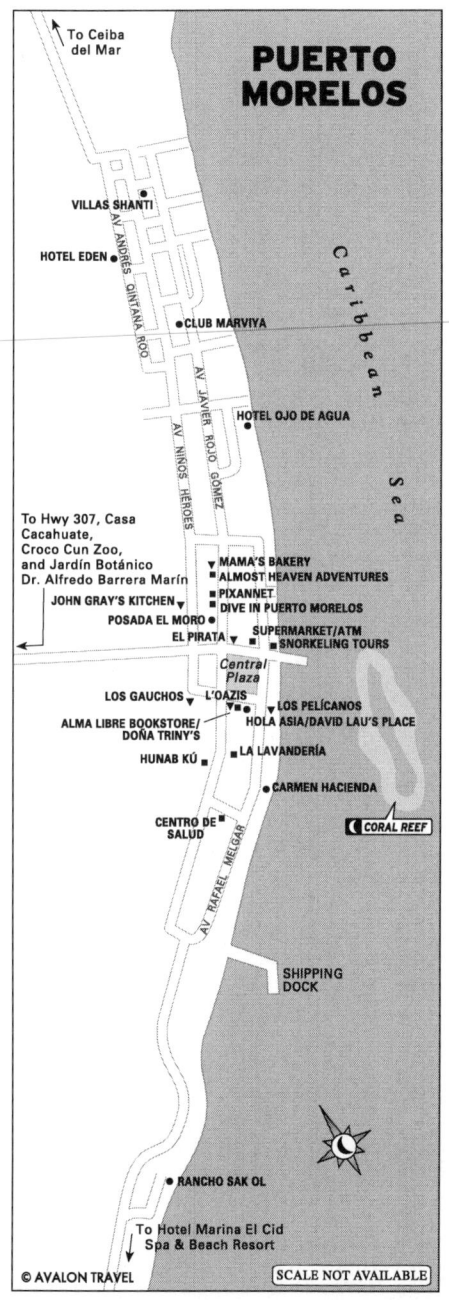

PUERTO MORELOS

To Ceiba del Mar

VILLAS SHANTI

HOTEL EDEN

AV. ANDRES QUINTANA ROO

CLUB MARVIYA

Caribbean Sea

AV. JAVIER ROJO GOMEZ

HOTEL OJO DE AGUA

AV. NIÑOS HEROES

To Hwy 307, Casa Cacahuate, Croco Cun Zoo, and Jardín Botánico Dr. Alfredo Barrera Marín

MAMA'S BAKERY
ALMOST HEAVEN ADVENTURES
PIXANNET
JOHN GRAY'S KITCHEN
DIVE IN PUERTO MORELOS
POSADA EL MORO
EL PIRATA
SUPERMARKET/ATM
SNORKELING TOURS

Central Plaza

LOS GAUCHOS
L'OAZIS
LOS PELÍCANOS
HOLA ASIA/DAVID LAU'S PLACE
ALMA LIBRE BOOKSTORE/ DOÑA TRINY'S
LA LAVANDERÍA
HUNAB KÚ

CARMEN HACIENDA

CENTRO DE SALUD

CORAL REEF

AV. RAFAEL MELGAR

SHIPPING DOCK

RANCHO SAK OL

To Hotel Marina El Cid Spa & Beach Resort

© AVALON TRAVEL

SCALE NOT AVAILABLE

THE RIVIERA MAYA

was harvested to be used in chewing gum), a few ruins from the Post-Classic period, and a contemporary Maya hut illustrating day-to-day life—from cooking facilities to hammocks. Wear long sleeves, pants, and closed-toe shoes, and definitely bring bug repellent—the mosquitoes can be fierce, especially in the late afternoon and after it rains.

SHOPPING

A so-called **Sunday Jungle Market** (Casa Cacahuate, Calle 2, Zona Urbana, 9:30 A.M.–2 P.M. Sun., Oct.–Aug. only) is held at Casa Cacahuate bed-and-breakfast in the residential part of Puerto Morelos, on the other side of the highway. This cheerful family-friendly event is facilitated by the nonprofit founded by the bed-and-breakfast's owners. The market includes a variety of handicrafts produced by local women, as well as tasty food and drink. A traditional Maya dance is held at 11:30 A.M.

The artisans' market of **Hunab Kú** (1.5 blocks south of the plaza, 9 A.M.–8 P.M. daily) may be your best bet for finding nice handicrafts. Here, you'll find a bunch of stands with colorful blankets, ceramics, hammocks, masks, jipi hats, shell art...pretty much anything you'll see sold up and down the coast.

The best and largest English-language bookstore on the peninsula, **Alma Libre Bookstore** (central plaza, tel. 998/871-0713, www.almalibrebooks.com, 10 A.M.–3 P.M. and 6–9 P.M. Mon.–Sat., 4–9 P.M. Sun., closed June–mid-Oct.) has a whopping 20,000 titles, ranging from "beach trash to Plato," in the words of the friendly Canadian owners. There's Maya culture, Mexican cooking, learning Spanish, bird-watching, snorkeling guides, classics, philosophy, mysteries, fiction, nonfiction—not just in English but Spanish, French, German, Dutch, Italian, Norwegian, and more—your taste in books would have to be extremely narrow to not find something you like here. Books are both new and used, and trade-ins (two for one) are accepted. The store also has a wide selection of guidebooks and maps; check the website for tons of additional information or sign up for their email newsletter.

SPORTS AND RECREATION
Snorkeling

Puerto Morelos is justly famous for its snorkeling, with a protected stretch of coral reef running very near shore. A **local cooperative** (8 A.M.–3 P.M. Mon.–Sat.) offers excellent and affordable tours, visiting two spots on the reef for 45 minutes apiece, and using boats with sunshades. Prices are fixed: US$25 per person, including equipment, park fees, and a bottle of water. Boats leave every 30 minutes from the municipal pier; if there are fewer than three people, you have to wait up to 30 minutes (but no more) for additional passengers to come. Sign up at the cooperative's kiosk at the northeast corner of the plaza; late morning is the best time to go, as the sun is high but the afternoon winds haven't started.

The dive shops in town also offer snorkeling tours. **Dive In Puerto Morelos** (Av. Javier Rojo Gómez 14, tel. 998/206-9084, www.diveinpuertomorelos.com, 8 A.M.–9 P.M. Mon.–Sat.) offers a tour similar to the cooperative's, while **Wet Set Water Adventures** (Hotel Ojo de Agua, tel. 998/871-0198, www.wetset.com, 8 A.M.–2 P.M. daily) offers outings of various lengths, from just one site (45 mins, US$16 pp) to three (2.5 hrs, US$26 pp). Prices include snorkel gear and park fee.

Caution: *Do not swim to the reef* from anywhere along the beach. Although it's close enough for strong swimmers to reach, boats use the channel between the reef and the shore, and tourists have been struck and killed in the past.

Scuba Diving

Puerto Morelos has over two dozen dive sites within a 15-minute boat ride, virtually all in protected marine reserve waters. Add to that the nearby cenotes, plus night and wreck diving, and divers have plenty to keep them happy and interested. The dive shops in town—there were three at last count—tend to have small groups, and offer a full range of fun dives and certification courses. Prices are fairly uniform—roughly US$50/70 for one/ two tanks, and US$400 for open-water certification—and always include equipment.

Reservations are strongly recommended in the high season.

Dive In Puerto Morelos (Av. Javier Rojo Gómez 14, tel. 998/206-9084, www.diveinpuertomorelos.com, 8 A.M.–9 P.M. Mon.–Sat.) is run by a friendly American dive instructor, emphasizing safety and small groups. It's a great choice for divers of all levels.

Wet Set Water Adventures (Hotel Ojo de Agua, tel. 998/871-0198, www.wetset.com, 8 A.M.–2 P.M. daily) is one of the longest-running dive shops around, offering top-to-bottom service—even rinsing your gear—and extensive area expertise.

Almost Heaven Adventures (Av. Javier Rojo Gómez, tel. 998/871-0230, www.almostheavenadventures.com, 8 A.M.–6 P.M. Mon.–Sat.) is the in-house shop at Ceiba del Mar hotel and spa, but also has a downtown location a half block from the center.

Sport Fishing

The dive shops in Puerto Morelos also offer fishing trips, whether trolling for barracuda or dorado (even marlin) or dropping a line for "dinner fish" like grouper or snapper. **Wet Set Water Adventures** (Hotel Ojo de Agua, tel. 998/871-0198, www.wetset.com, 8 A.M.–2 P.M. daily) has the most experience and even guarantees you'll catch fish or the trip is free. Trips typically cost US$215–300 for 2–4 people and 4–5 hours, and US$50–60 per additional hour.

ATV Excursions

Puerto Morelos Adventure (Hotel Ojo de Agua, tel. 998/884-2314, www.puertomorelosadventure.com, 8 A.M.–6 P.M. daily) offers a four-hour ATV tour (US$58 pp double, US$68 single) that weaves through sand dunes and coastal forest with stops at two cenotes to cool off. One cenote has a zip line for a bit of a rush. A bilingual guide and light lunch at Hotel Ojo de Agua (Av. Javier Rojo Gómez near Ejército Mexicano) are usually included.

Tours

Ecab Explorer (tel. 998/123-5062, http://

ekaabts.spaces.live.com) is a one-man tour operation launched by a longtime Puerto Morelos resident (and former purveyor of fine shrimp tacos). Among various recommended tours are Dos Aguas (Two Waters, US$55 pp, 4 hrs), which includes snorkeling on the ocean reef and a nearby freshwater cenote, and Cobá Maya, in which you visit Cobá ruins plus a nearby Maya village and monkey reserve (US$125 pp, 9 hrs); check the website for details on these and other options. Groups tend to be small and the service highly personalized; transportation, entrance fees, and lunch and/ or soft drinks are all included.

Located four kilometers (2.5 miles) south of Puerto Morelos **Loma Bonita** (Carr. Cancún–Chetumal Km 42.5, tel. 998/887-5465, www.rancholomabonita.com, US$65 adults, US$57 children under 12) is the Riviera Maya's longest-running horseback riding operation. Tours last two hours and include horseback riding along the beach, in the jungle, and into the ocean (or, if you prefer, you can just hang out on the beach instead). Drinks, snacks, and accident insurance are included in the rate. Tours start at 9 A.M., noon, and 3 P.M.; reservations are recommended and be sure to arrive at least 30 minutes before the tour begins. ATV tours (2 hrs, US$65, US$51 pp shared) and wave runner tours (40 mins, US$60.50, US$50 pp shared) also offered. Round-trip transportation, including to and from Cancún, is an additional US$15 per person.

Spa

The **Jungle Spa** (Casa Cacahuate, Calle 2, Zona Urbana, tel. 998/208-9148, www.mayaecho.com) is one of several community projects undertaken by Lu'um K'aa Nab, a nonprofit run by the owners of Casa Cacahuate. Local women provide professional massage and traditional Maya treatments, for far less than at ordinary spas. Treat yourself to one of various available treatments, from a four-handed full-body massage (US$70, 1 hr) to a deluxe facial including head and neck massage (US$25, 45 mins). Group massage or *temescal* (traditional Maya sweat lodge) can also be arranged, with advance notice.

ACCOMMODATIONS

Under US$50

Hotel Eden (Av. Andrés Quintana Roo No. 788, tel. 998/871-0450, US$45 s/d, US$55 s/d with a/c) may not be the paradise its name suggests, but makes a good budget option all the same. Decor and flair are in short supply—not to mention TVs—but the spacious studios do have ceiling fans, clean hot-water bathrooms, and small kitchenettes. The kitchens aren't equipped (strangely) but the friendly proprietors usually have some extra pots and pans to loan you. The hotel is located on a quiet street just two blocks from the beach.

Casa Cacahuate (Calle 2, Zona Urbana, tel. 998/208-9148, www.mayaecho.com, US$30 s, US$50 d, breakfast included) is a charming bed-and-breakfast located in Puerto Morelos's "urban zone," the residential area on the inland side of the highway, offering a rare opportunity to experience the non-touristed side of the Riviera Maya. Homey even by bed-and-breakfast standards, the house has two tidy guest rooms upstairs and the personable owners below, all sharing a *palapa*-covered terrace, outdoor sitting area, and ample gardens with enticing hammocks and chairs. The owners maintain close ties with the community, and host a popular crafts market and Jungle Spa on-site. The beach and central plaza are a bit of a hike—the main drawback to staying here—but taxis are plentiful if needed.

US$50-100

(Posada El Moro (Av. Javier Rojo Gómez, tel. 998/871-0159, www.posadaelmoro.com, US$50 s/d, US$55 s/d with a/c, US$60 s/d with a/c and TV, US$75 suite with kitchenette) is one of Puerto Morelos's most charming hotels, and a great deal to boot. Operated by a friendly English-speaking family and located just a half block from the main square, El Moro has 10 brightly painted units with polished cement floors, comfortable beds, and plenty of natural light. There's free wireless Internet in the lobby and a pleasant little pool in back that's perfect for cooling off on a hot afternoon. Fresh coffee is available to guests every morning.

Still known by some repeat visitors as Rancho Libertad, 【 **Rancho Sak Ol** (1 km/0.6 mi south of the central plaza, tel. 998/871-0181, www.ranchosakol.com, US$75 s with a/c, US$85 d with a/c, US$110–120 suite with fan and 2-night minimum) is a relaxing *palapa* hideaway a short distance south of town. Rooms have hanging beds—which are actually quite stable—and individual patios with hammocks. Downstairs units have air-conditioning, while upstairs rooms have cross-breezes. A large buffet breakfast is included, and guests can use the community kitchen; for eating out, the town is an easy 15-minute walk away. The beach here is just okay—very clean, with good snorkeling offshore, but with rather thin sand and boxed in by the cargo ferry on one side and a huge condo complex on the other. Still, there's enough breathing room so as not to spoil Rancho Sak Ol's quiet, isolated feel. The resort is for adults only, except during the low season when children over the age of 10 are welcome. The use of snorkel equipment and bicycles is also included in the rate.

The wine-red **Club Marviya** (Av. Javier Rojo Gómez s/n, three blocks north of the central plaza, tel. 998/871-0049, Canada tel. 450/492-9094, www.marviya.com, US$75 s/d with breakfast included, US$90 studio) is a laid-back Quebecois and Mexican-run place with six rooms and a communal kitchen, plus larger studio apartments a short distance away. The hotel rooms, all on the 2nd floor of a converted mansion just a few steps from the beach, have firm beds, ceramic floors, and terrific views (and cool sea breezes) from small terraces. The studios are spacious and tidy. Bikes and beach gear can be rented or borrowed; look for deep discounts in the off-season.

Hotel Ojo de Aqua (Av. Javier Rojo Gómez, two blocks north of plaza, tel. 998/871-0027, www.ojo-de-agua.com, US$70–100 s/d) offers 36 basic rooms overlooking a pretty beach. Standard and deluxe rooms come with cable TV and air-conditioning; the former are a bit cramped. Studio units have a refrigerator, stove, sink, and fans, but no air-conditioning. All are clean and comfortable, though lacking in character—the flowered bedspreads and tile floors are classic hotel room. Families will appreciate the large protected pool area, and there is a dive shop and tour operator on-site for snorkeling, diving, kayaking, and ATV tours.

US$100-150

A block from the beach, **Villas Shanti** (Av. Niños Héroes s/n, tel. 998/871-0040, www .villasshanti.com, US$140 s/d with a/c) offers eight one-bedroom units, each with a modern bathroom, fully equipped kitchenette, and private patio; all face a sunny courtyard that has a clover-shaped pool and a large *palapa* with hammocks. A spacious two-bedroom villa with full kitchen, living room, and dining room is also available for four to six guests (from US$2,240/ week). Yoga workshops and retreats are regularly held here—classes are in a bright indoor studio or a large *palapa* in the garden.

One block south of the plaza, **Carmen Hacienda** (Av. Rafael Melgar, tel. 998/871-0448, www.carmeninn.com, US$90–130 s/d with a/c) is a reinvention of a longtime Puerto Morelos hotel, the Hacienda Morales, and is part of a small family of hotels based in Playa del Carmen. The rooms remain bright and spacious, with kitchens and ocean views, while new decoration and furnishings, including mini-air-conditioners and wireless Internet, give it a much-needed update. A sunny (though somewhat artless) patio with a small pool separates the hotel from the beach, and there's a decent restaurant on-site.

Over US$150

Ceiba del Mar (1.5 km/0.9 mi north of town, tel. 998/872-8060, toll-free Mex. tel. 800/426-9772, toll-free U.S. tel. 877/545-6221, www.ceibadelmar.com, US$399 s/d with a/c, US$447–765 suite, US$1,024 penthouse) offers a high-end resort experience with a laid-back vibe. Located in eight three-story stucco buildings, the units are elegantly appointed and have the modern amenities you'd expect like flat-screen TVs with DVD, CD players, and minibars. Continental breakfast is included and is served in-room through a butler box—you won't even have to throw on your robe to open the door. The resort also boasts two glorious pools, a full-service spa and gym, two restaurants, a dive shop, and tennis courts with lights. The resort offers complimentary use of snorkel gear, kayaks, and bikes. **Hotel Marina El Cid Spa & Beach Resort** (Blvd. El Cid Unidad 15, tel. 998/872-8999, toll-free U.S./Canada tel. 866/306-6113, www.elcid.com, US$460–525 d) is Puerto Morelos's first all-inclusive resort—a milestone that didn't please everyone in this tightly knit town. It's fairly small by Riviera Maya standards, but far larger than anything else in Puerto Morelos, and many complained about damage to the mangroves and reef. The resort gets high marks from families, with a kid's club, waterslide, and manageable size, though the beach is smallish and often littered with coral fragments. Rooms have modern tasteful decor, and larger units have two full bathrooms, kitchen, and/or en-suite hot tubs. The hotel is located well south of town, though complimentary bicycles are available, and they organize club crawls in Cancún.

FOOD

Who knows how it happened, but unassuming Puerto Morelos has an amazingly rich collection of restaurants and eateries, from cheerful holes-in-the-wall to international cuisine rivaling anything in Cancún or Playa del Carmen.

Mexican and Seafood

El Pirata (central plaza, tel. 998/871-0489, 8 A.M.–11 P.M. Mon.–Thurs., until 2 A.M. Fri.–Sun., US$5–15) has a good location on the central plaza just up from the pier where you take snorkeling tours. Choose from a large selection of hamburgers, fish burgers, *tortas,* tacos, and full entrées such as roast chicken or grilled beef, all served in a simple open-air dining area just off the street. Like many businesses here, El Pirata cuts back its hours in the low season, closing Mondays and the entire month of May.

Doña Triny's (central plaza, 8 A.M.–11 P.M daily, US$4–9) started out as a tiny shack at the entrance of town, and now occupies prime property on the main plaza, rubbing elbows with the likes of Hola Asia and the Alma Libre bookstore. Neither the low-key ambience nor the familiar menu have changed much; look for Mexican and Yucatecan standards like enchiladas, huaraches, and chile rellenos, plus some adopted dishes like stuffed portobello mushrooms; most dishes can be adjusted for vegetarians on request. Live music is planned for Friday and Saturday nights.

Los Pelícanos (central plaza, tel. 998/871-0014, 8 A.M.–10:30 P.M. daily, US$7–20) has a wraparound patio overlooking the plaza and the ocean—perfect for an afternoon beer or margarita. Food here can be a bit uneven, but with so many anglers in town it's hard to go wrong with shrimp, octopus, or fish, all served fresh in a half dozen different ways.

International

▮ John Gray's Kitchen (Av. Niños Héroes, half block north of plaza, tel. 998/871-0665, 6–10 P.M. Mon.–Sat., US$17–30) is the sister restaurant of John Gray's Place in Playa del Carmen, and without question the finest restaurant in Puerto Morelos. The menu changes virtually every day, though a few perennial favorites are almost always available, like the soy-marinated tuna appetizer and the honey-chipotle duck entrée. Fine cuts of meat, inventive sauces, and fresh pastas and vegetables are a given. Occupying a boxy building two blocks from the plaza, the dining room is elegant and understated and the service is excellent. They only take cash.

Giving John Gray's Place a run for its culinary money is **▮ Hola Asia** (central plaza, tel. 998/871-0679, 3–11 P.M. Mon.–Sat., 1–10 P.M. Sun., closed Sept., US$8–15), a small, popular restaurant serving a terrific pan-Asian menu of mostly Thai and Chinese inspiration. Diners come from Cancún, Playa del Carmen, and beyond to eat here, and the restaurant has added a rooftop patio to accommodate the crowds. For sweet and sour, try General Tso's Chicken; for spicy go with Indian Yellow Curry.

David Lau's Place (central plaza, tel. 998/251-2531, www.davidlaus.com, 3–11 P.M. Mon.–Tues. and Thurs.–Sat., 1–10 P.M. Sun., US$8–15) was opened by the former chef at Hola Asia, and also serves terrific Asian-inspired dishes, plus a handful of select Italian dishes. Dishes are made to order and served at lovely indoor and outdoor tables; portions tend to be enormous.

There's great homemade pizza and pasta at **Los Gauchos** (Calle Tulum, tel. 998/871-0475, 2–10 P.M. Wed.–Sun., US$5–8), but don't leave without trying the empanadas: a classic Argentinean snack made of puffy, crispy fried dough filled with cheese or other goodies. At just US$1.50 apiece, a plate of five or six and a couple of sodas makes a great cheap meal for two. Take them to go or eat at one of a few small tables on the sidewalk.

The Quebecois owners of **L'Oazis** (www.loazis.com, 5–10 P.M. Tues.–Sun., US$7–15) serve mostly grilled dishes in their small, cheerful eatery. The menu includes tacos, burgers, and New York steak, plus specialties like zucchini and eggplant with tzatziki sauce.

Light Fare

A Puerto Morelos institution, **◖ Mama's Bakery** (Av. Javier Rojo Gómez, one block north of plaza, cell tel. 044-998/845-6810, 7:30 A.M.–2 P.M. Tues.–Sat., sometimes Sun., US$4–6) is run by a friendly expat and baker extraordinaire. The sticky buns and carrot cake are irresistible, and there's a waiting list for fresh loaves of bread—order at least a day in advance. Mama's also serves fresh tasty meals, like pancakes or breakfast burritos in the morning and smoothies and sandwiches for lunch. The restaurant is typically closed on weekends after Labor Day until November 1.

Groceries

The supermarket (north side of the central plaza, 6 A.M.–10 P.M. daily) has a fairly large selection of canned foods, pastas, snacks, and drinks, and has a small produce section near the back.

INFORMATION AND SERVICES

Although this town sees a fair number of tourists, the services remain somewhat sparse.

Emergency Services

The modest **Centro de Salud** (no phone, 8 A.M.–2:30 P.M. daily) is south of the plaza, on an unmarked connector street between Avenidas Javier Rojo Gómez and Rafael Melgar. While fine for minor issues, any serious medical issues should be attended to in Cancún or Playa del Carmen.

Money

There is no bank in Puerto Morelos, but there's an HSBC ATM just outside the supermarket on the plaza's north side.

Media and Communications

Next door to Dive In Puerto Morelos, **PixanNET** (Av. Javier Rojo Gómez, tel. 998/206-9275, 9 A.M.–4 P.M. and 6–10 P.M. Mon.–Sat.) has a fast Internet connection for US$1.50 per hour. You can also download and burn your digital photos to a CD here for around US$2. Calls to the United States and Canada are US$0.30 a minute.

Laundry

A block south of the plaza, the aptly named **La Lavandería** (Av. Javier Rojo Gómez s/n, no phone, 8 A.M.–8 P.M. Mon.–Sat.) charges US$1.40 per kilogram (2.2 pounds) to wash, dry, and fold your dirty duds (minimum 2 kilograms/4.4 pounds).

GETTING THERE AND AROUND

Puerto Morelos is 36 kilometers (22 miles) south of Cancún and even closer to the airport, just 18 kilometers (11 miles). The town itself is compact enough that you can probably manage without a car (unless you're staying at Ceiba del Mar or possibly Rancho Sak Ol). That said, having a vehicle makes exploring the Riviera Maya beyond Puerto Morelos significantly easier.

Europcar (Calle Tulum, tel. 998/206-9372, www.europcar.com.mx, 8 A.M.–1 P.M. and

2–6 P.M. daily) has a small office just off the main plaza, making it the most convenient option for renting a car. Otherwise, Cancún airport has a large number of agencies, and you can often find excellent deals online.

Bus

ADO buses pass the Puerto Morelos turnoff on Hwy. 307, but do not enter town. The northbound stop is right at the turnoff, while the southbound bus stop is across the street and a block south. For Cancún (US$1.50–2, 45 mins) and Playa del Carmen (US$1.50–2, 35 mins), second-class buses and *combis* (shared vans) pass every 10 minutes 6 A.M.–1 A.M. daily, and less frequently throughout the night. Some go as far as Tulum (US$4.50–6.50, 1.5 hrs), but you should double-check before getting on. Buses to the **Cancún Airport** (US$4.50, 25 mins) pass roughly every hour from 7:35 A.M. to 7:55 P.M. daily.

Taxi

Taxis line up day and night at the taxi stand on the northwest corner of the central plaza. Prices are fixed and prominently displayed on a signboard at the taxi stand. A ride to the highway costs around US$2.

PUNTA BETE AND PLAYA XCALACOCO

It used to be that the only way to find Punta Bete and its main beach, Playa Xcalacoco, was to look for the big Cristal water plant. That's still the best landmark, but a flurry of new construction, and renovation of existing locations, has prompted hoteliers to finally add signs along the highway as well. The beach here is decent—the sand is clean but coarse, and the shoreline rocky in places—but the snorkeling is good and the isolation has always been a big plus. It's still a quiet place, but all the new development—including a huge condo complex—may mark a new chapter for this long-overlooked stretch of beach.

Accommodations

Hotel Petit Lafitte (tel. 984/877-4000, www.petitlafitte.com, US$250–350 s/d with a/c) offers the comfort of a full-scale hotel on this isolated stretch of beach, including a large pool, plenty of poolside lounge space, and a well-maintained beach area with *palapas* and hammocks. Accommodations are either in the main building, where all the rooms have at least partial ocean views, or in spacious beachfront bungalows. All accommodations have one or two beds, cable TV, air-conditioning, minibar, and Wi-Fi. Rates include a full breakfast and dinner for two.

Coco's Cabañas (tel. 998/880-5629, www.tulumresorts.com, US$85 s/d) has a handful of charming *palapa*-roof bungalows on a small garden plot. The *cabañas* are comfortable and clean, and have private patios with hammocks. There's a heart-shaped pool next to the open-air dining area and bar, and the beach is just 30 meters (100 feet) away. Be sure to call in advance for a room—there isn't always staff on-site.

Food

Coco's Cabañas (tel. 998/880-5629, www.tulumresorts.com/Riviera-Maya/Coco-s-Cabanas/, 11 A.M.–10 P.M. daily, US$5–18) has a small outdoor bar and restaurant, serving dishes you don't often see in these parts, like fish-and-chips, blackened rib eye, and banana flambé.

Getting There and Around

From the highway, follow the access road two kilometers (1.2 miles) until it forks at the Tides Riviera Maya resort. Bear left to reach the hotels and beach.

There is no taxi stand in this tiny community; when guests need one, hotels call cabs from Playa del Carmen or Puerto Morelos. A ride to the airport costs US$40, to Playa del Carmen around US$10.

Playa del Carmen

Playa del Carmen (or Playa for short) has long been a favorite among travelers looking for an alternative to Cancún, a place where boutique hotels and cool lounge bars outnumber glitzy high-rises and all-night clubs. Playa's tourist and residential areas are more intertwined than Cancún's, and it's easier to find "authentic" Mexican outlets, especially compared to the Cancún Zona Hotelera. And while Cancún is an American playground, Playa attracts mostly Europeans, and even has a nascent Italian quarter.

But Playa is no longer the quaint seaside village many remember. Its population has exploded in recent years (as much as 20 percent per year), making it one of the fastest-growing cities in the region and country. It wasn't too long ago that Playa's main tourist strip—Quinta Avenida, or 5th Avenue—was just a half dozen blocks long; now it stretches more than 20 blocks and grows longer every year. Condos are popping up seemingly everywhere, and the southern end of Playa (the part nearest

the bus terminal and ferry terminal) has been almost completely overtaken by kitschy stores and chain restaurants—and in that way is little different than the over-commercialized parts of Cancún.

Fortunately, Playa still has plenty of small hotels, funky charm, and offbeat shops, especially in the middle and northern sections of Quinta Avenida, to help it remain a true alternative to Cancún. It's got some great beaches (if you know where to look) and the atmosphere remains decidedly mellow, even with all the changes. Playa's central location also makes it a convenient base from which to explore the rest of the Riviera Maya and Yucatán Peninsula, whether snorkeling in cenotes, diving on Isla Cozumel, or visiting inland Maya ruins.

SIGHTS
◖ Quinta Avenida

Playa's main pedestrian and commercial drag is Quinta Avenida, or 5th Avenue, which stretches more than 20 blocks from the ferry

Open-air restaurants and funky shops await on Playa's very own 5th Avenue.

© LIZA PRADO

dock northward. Pronounced KEEN-ta av-en-EE-da, you may see it written as 5 Avenida or 5a Avenida—5a is akin to 5th in English. The first several blocks, especially around the ferry dock, are typical tourist traps, with souvenir shops and chain restaurants. Around Calle 10 or Calle 12, the atmosphere turns mellower, with bistros, jazz bars, and funky clothing stores. The section north of Avenida Constituyentes is cool and youthful, and is known as Little Italy for the number of Italian restaurants and Italian-owned shops there. You'll probably walk the length of Quinta Avenida once or twice—the best beaches are in the northern part, the bus terminal and ferry dock in the southern—and everyone seems to find his or her favorite part.

Beaches and Beach Clubs

With thick white sand and mild surf, **Playa Tukán** (entrance at 1 Av. Norte at Calle 26) has long been the best beach in town. There used to be a long stretch of "unclaimed" beach where anyone could stake out a patch of sand and sun for the day. Today, condo developments have gobbled up large sections of shore, and a handful of beach clubs cover much of the rest. The latter are open to the public so there's no question of being able to relax and enjoy the beach; it's just that you'll probably end up renting lounge chairs and an umbrella rather than laying out your towel somewhere. On the bright side, beach clubs have bar and restaurant service, showers, lockers, and in some cases, small swimming pools. There are also small tour operators on Playa Tukán that offer snorkeling tours, Hobie Cat trips, kayaks, and more.

Playa Tukán's beach clubs are each a little different, appealing more or less to different types of beachgoers. Generally speaking, **Club Tukán** (8 A.M.–6 P.M. daily) and **Chiquitita** (8 A.M.–6 P.M. daily) are mellow and good for families, while **Mamita's** (9 A.M.–6 P.M. daily) and **Nuddy Beach** (8 A.M.–6 P.M. daily) draw a younger, hipper set with techno music and beach beds. Prices are fairly uniform: around US$2–4 a day for chairs and umbrellas,

US$8–15 for beach beds and large *palapas,* and US$5–15 for snacks and drinks.

Playa El Faro (btwn. Calles 8 and 10) is an excellent beach just steps from the action on Quinta Avenida. Named for the large lighthouse *(faro)* at one end, it still has plenty of room to lay out your towel, unlike other stretches that have been snatched by encroaching hotels. Jaime's Marina (Playa El Faro, end of Calle 10, tel. 984/130-2034, www.jaimesmarina.bravehost.com, 9 A.M.–5 P.M. daily), a well-recommended snorkel and sailing outfit, is located here.

Coco Maya Beach Club (end of Calle 12, 8 A.M.–6 P.M.) is a small low-key beach club that's easy to reach thanks to an adjacent public access path. The club's kitchen serves straightforward beach grub, and lounge chairs and beach beds are available for rent (US$5–20/day).

Coco Beach Club (8 A.M.–6 P.M. daily) is just a short distance north of Shangri La Caribe. It has good food, beach umbrellas, and sun beds, plus changing rooms and showers. The snorkeling here is the best in the Playa area, and there's gear for rent if you don't have your own.

Xcaret Ecopark

Just five kilometers (three miles) south of Playa, Xcaret (Hwy. 307 Km. 282, toll-free Mex. tel. 800/292-2738, www.xcaret.com .mx, 8:30 A.M.–9 P.M. daily, US$69/34.50 adult/child, US$99/49.50 adult/child including snorkeling equipment, buffet, and snack) is a mega-ecopark offering water activities like snorkeling in underground rivers and swimming with dolphins and sharks; up-close animal viewing areas including jaguar and puma islands, a butterfly pavilion, and an aquarium; and spectacular shows, like a Maya ball game, regional dance, and music performances. Beyond this, the park is also dedicated to protecting the region's flora and fauna; there are breeding areas for scarlet macaws and turtles, a section dedicated to the endemic stingerless bee, and an orchid greenhouse—all with educational exhibits for visitors. If you're into

THE RIVIERA MAYA

THE RIVIERA M

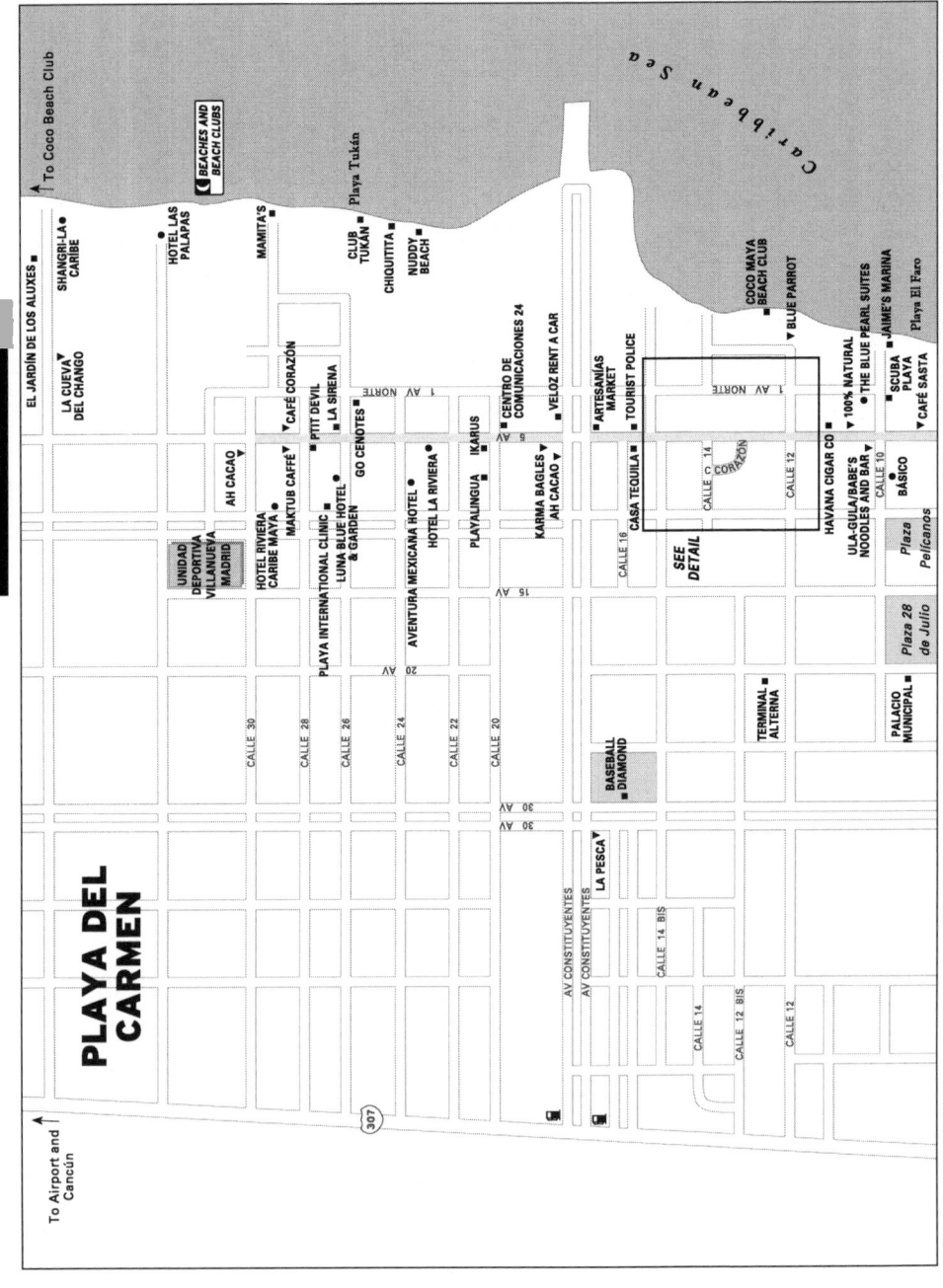

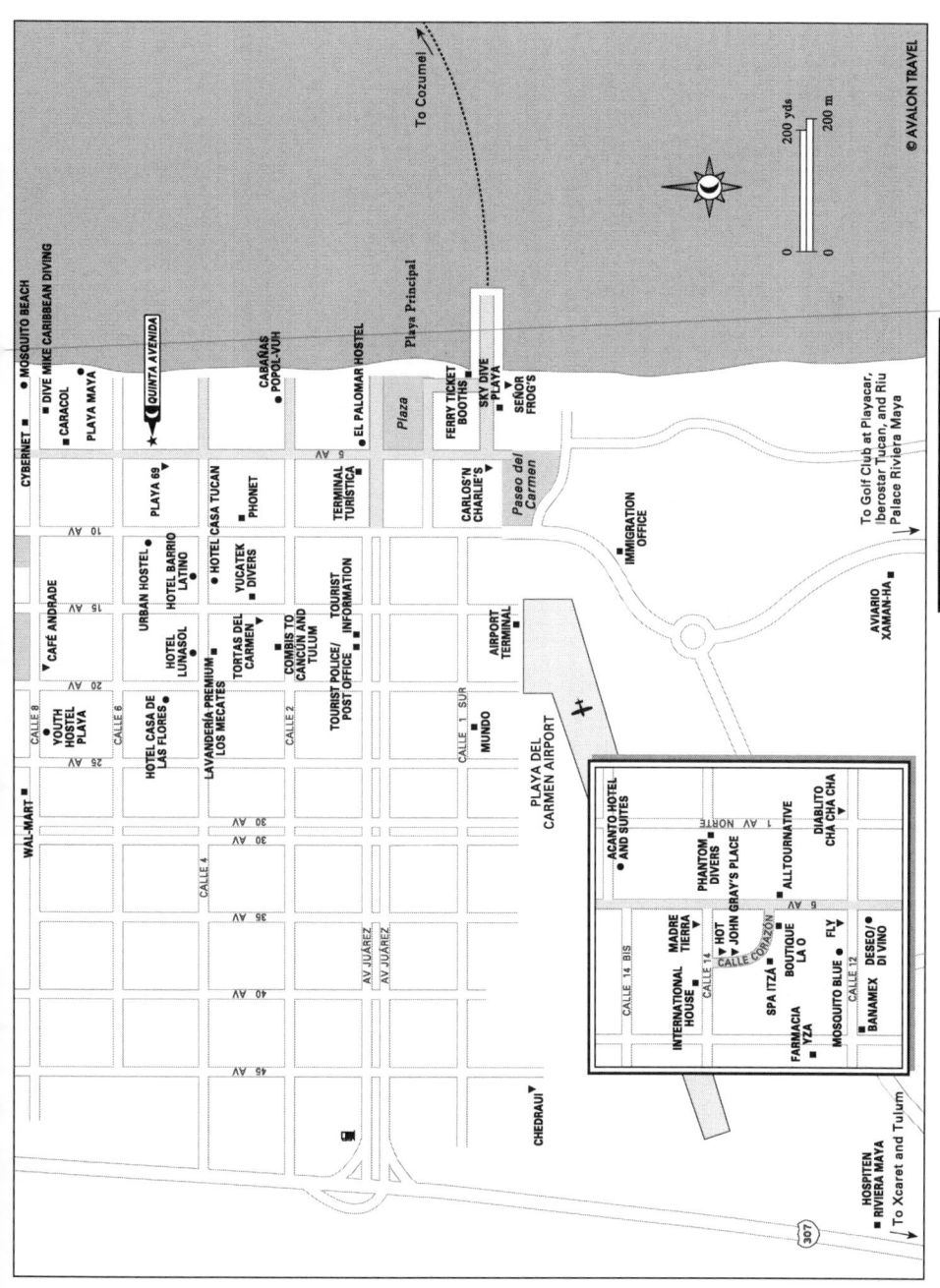

© AVALON TRAVEL

© LIZA PRADO

Xcaret is a huge ecopark and a fun all-day outing with something for everyone.

organized activities or are traveling with kids, this is definitely a worthwhile stop. (Get 10 percent off if you book online.)

Aviario Xaman-Ha

A short distance inside the Playacar entrance off 10 Avenida, this bird sanctuary (Av. Xaman Ha, 9 A.M.–5 P.M. daily, US$15 adult, children under 12 free) has more than 60 species of tropical birds, including toucans, flamingos, cormorants, and various types of parrots, all native to southeastern Mexico. The birds are divided by habitat and held in a variety of enclosures along a winding path—most people take a little less than an hour to see them all. Bring bug repellent, especially if you visit in the late afternoon or after it rains.

ENTERTAINMENT AND EVENTS

Playa del Carmen doesn't have the wild nightclubs that Cancún does, nor would many of the people who visit regularly want it to. But Playa does boast a great bar and lounge scene, and you'll find plenty of lively spots along Quinta

Avenida just about any night of the week. An emerging hot spot is at and around the corner of 1 Avenida and Calle 12, where the Blue Parrot, an oldie but goody, has been joined by a handful of newer bars, and you can dance from one to the next well into the wee hours.

Bars and Nightclubs

One of Playa's classic hot spots, the **Blue Parrot** (Calle 12 at the beach, tel. 984/206-3350, www.blueparrot.com, 7:30 A.M.–4 A.M. daily, no cover) is still going strong with a crowd most nights. Sand floors, swing bar seats, a candlelit *palapa* lounge, and a small dance floor all create the party feel that have kept customers streaming in for years. DJs play everything from retro to techno; be sure to check out the fire dancers, nightly at 11 P.M.

With retro tables and armchairs, and low beats and even lower lights, **Diablito Cha Cha Cha** (1 Av. at Calle 12, tel. 984/803-3695, 1 P.M.–3 A.M. daily) is certainly the most stylish of the bars and clubs in this up-and-coming area. Order anything under the sun from the bar, and munch on unlikely Mexican-Japanese fusion snacks and meals.

DJs spin urban beats at **Deseo** (5 Av. at Calle 12, tel. 984/879-3620, www.hoteldeseo.com, 5 P.M.–12:30 A.M. daily), a sleek minimalist lounge bar that attracts local and foreign hipsters most nights of the week. Part of a like-named hotel, the rooftop lounge is the centerpiece of the place; a candlelit stone stairway leads to a pool surrounded by queen-size cushions and billowing curtains.

The scene is mellow and relaxed at **Di Vino** (5 Av. at Calle 12, 4 P.M.–2 A.M. daily), an upscale by-the-glass wine bar right on the main drag. The wine menu is large and reasonably sophisticated, and it's also open during the day as a restaurant.

One of Playa's only gay bars, **Playa 69** (off 5 Av. between Calles 4 and 6, tel. 984/876-9466, 9 P.M.–4 A.M. daily) is hopping on weekends, when tequila shots are almost mandatory. Popular with locals, the entrance is kind of hard to spot—follow the rainbow sign down an alley on the west side of Quinta Avenida.

The beach club **Nuddy Beach** (Playa Tukán) turns into a lounge bar Thursday–Saturday nights (7 P.M.–3 A.M., no cover) with mellow, modern music and a cool attitude so thick you can cut it with a knife. On Thursdays women drink for free, and Saturday's Sunset Party features two-for-one champagne and wine.

And of course you can always find a party at **Señor Frog's** (ferry pier, 10 A.M.–1 A.M. daily) and **Carlos'n Charlie's** (Paseo del Carmen, southern end of 5 Av., tel. 984/803-3498, 10 A.M.–1 A.M. daily), both near the Cozumel ferry pier. These bars are a fixture in Mexican beach towns and are famous for their yard-long drinks, dancing on the tables, and non-stop parties.

SHOPPING

Playa del Carmen offers some of the best shopping on the Riviera Maya and Quinta Avenida is where it's at. You'll find everything from high-end clothing, gorgeous *artesanía*, Cuban cigars, and specialty tequila to jewelry, T-shirts,

and postcard stands. You name it, Playa del Carmen probably has it.

Artesanía

La Sirena (5 Av. at Calle 26, tel. 984/803-3422, 9 A.M.–10 P.M. daily) is a boutique specializing in Mexican folk art. Italian shop owner Patrizia personally selects the exceptional pieces—whimsical skeleton art, colonial statuettes of La Virgen de Guadalupe, tin-framed mirrors, bright shawls—you're sure to find something you can't resist.

Caracol (5 Av. btwn. Calles 6 and 8, tel. 984/803-1504, 9:30 A.M.–10:30 P.M. daily) is a pricey boutique selling unique Mexican textiles. It makes a great stop, even if just to admire the spectacular fabrics—clothing, tablecloths, bedding, and decorative art—that the German owner handpicks herself on buying trips throughout southern Mexico.

Bookstores

The best bookshop in the region is in nearby Puerto Morelos, and a stop there can be part of a nice day trip from Playa. In town, **Mundo** (Calle 1 Sur btwn. 20 and 25 Av., tel. 984/879-3004, www.pequemundo.com.mx, 9 A.M.–8 P.M. Mon.–Fri., 10 A.M.–6 P.M. Sat.) has several cases of English-language titles, new and used. Mysteries, romances, and other beach reads abound, but a close look turns up some good novels and nonfiction books. Prices run US$2–12, and the shop will buy the book back for 50 percent, cash or trade. You'll also find a small selection of regional maps.

Specialty Items

For a decent selection of specialty tequilas, check out **Casa Tequila** (5 Av. near Calle 14 Bus., 9 A.M.–midnight daily), where in addition to fine tequila you'll find a nice variety of silver jewelry. A small sister store is also at Quinta Avenida at Calle 16.

For the best in cigars, stop by **Havana Cigar Co.** (5 Av. btwn. Calles 10 and 12, tel. 984/803-1047, 9 A.M.–11:30 P.M. daily). Cuban and Mexican *puros* are sold individually (US$5–15) or by the box (US$55–450).

For boho beachwear, head to **Boutique La O** (Calle Corazón at 5 Av., tel. 984/803-3171, 9:30 A.M.–10:30 P.M. daily), where you'll find tie-dyed dresses, flowing linen pants, and cool cotton tops that are very comfy, and very Playa.

Shopping Centers

At the southern end of Quinta Avenida, **Paseo del Carmen** (10 A.M.–10 P.M. daily) is a shady outdoor shopping center with high-end clothing boutiques, jewelry stores, art galleries, and restaurants. Its series of modern fountains make it an especially pleasant place to window-shop, or enjoy an upscale lunch, after a morning at the beach.

For trinkets to take home, check out the **outdoor market** at the corner of Quinta Avenida and Constituyentes (8 A.M.–10 P.M. daily). You'll find everything from Maya pyramid key chains to silver jewelry.

SPORTS AND RECREATION
Scuba Diving

Playa del Carmen has decent offshore diving—virtually all drift dives, thanks to prevailing currents—and relatively easy access to Cozumel and inland cenotes. It's a logical base if you want a taste of all three, plus the convenience of being in town. However, if diving is the main reason you came, consider basing yourself on Cozumel itself, or closer to the cenotes, such as at Akumal or Tulum. This will save you the time, money, and effort of going back and forth.

Diving prices in Playa del Carmen are reasonable, and fairly uniform from shop to shop. Two-tank reef dives cost US$65–80, Cozumel trips and cenote trips are around US$100–150, and open-water certification courses run US$350–400. Gear is included in the courses, but is often charged separately for fun dives (US$15–20 per day). Most shops do not include the price of taking the ferry to Cozumel (US$20 round-trip), and additional fees, like marine park and cenote admissions, may also apply.

Tank-Ha Dive Center (Calle 10 btwn. 5 and 10 Avs., tel. 984/873-0302, www.tankha.com,

8 A.M.–10 P.M. daily) is one of the longest-operating shops in Playa, and a PADI Gold Palm resort and instructor training facility.

Dive Mike Caribbean Diving (Calle 8 btwn. 5 Av. and the beach, tel. 984/803-1228, www.divemike.com, 8 A.M.–10 P.M. daily) is a very friendly, professional, and reasonably priced shop. Check out its excellent and informative website for additional info and pictures.

Phantom Divers (1 Av. Norte at Calle 14, tel. 984/879-3988, www.phantomdivers.com, 8 A.M.–7 P.M. daily) is one of a handful of locally owned dive shops, offering friendly service and lower-than-average prices. No credit cards are accepted.

Yucatek Divers (15 Av. btwn. Calles 2 and 4, tel. 984/803-2836, www.yucatek-divers.com, 7:30 A.M.–6 P.M. daily) uses a neighboring hotel's pool for beginner certification training, and most fun dives are led by instructors.

Go Cenotes (1 Av. Norte btwn. Calles 24 and 26, tel. 984/876-2629, www.gocenotes.com, 8 A.M.–8 P.M. daily) specializes in cave and cavern trips and courses for divers of all levels. Groups are always small (1–4 people) and the shop works hard to be sure you dive different cenotes every time.

Scuba Playa (Calle 10 btwn. 1 and 5 Avs., tel. 984/803-3123, www.scubaplaya.com, 8 A.M.–8 P.M. daily) specializes in small groups and offers a six-dive package that includes two tanks apiece in Cozumel, the cenotes, and the reef.

Snorkeling

In Playa itself it's best to go snorkeling with a tour, since the snorkeling off the beach isn't too rewarding. There are also numerous cenotes near Playa that make for unique snorkeling, including several you can visit on your own.

Most of Playa's dive shops offer guided snorkeling tours to excellent sites. Ocean trips cost US$30–40, while cenote trips are US$50–60, all gear included. Be sure to ask how many people will be on the trip, how long the trip will last, and how many reefs you'll be visiting (for ocean trips). For cenote trips, we strongly recommend a wetsuit, even if it means renting one for a few extra bucks. The water is quite chilly, there's no sun, and you'll be better protected against cuts and scrapes.

Jaime's Marina (Playa El Faro, end of Calle 10, tel. 984/130-2034, www.jaimesmarina .bravehost.com, 9 A.M.–5 P.M. daily) is just a kiosk on the beach, but it offers friendly service and good snorkeling tours, among a number of water activities. Snorkel trips (US$35, two hrs) include an hour of snorkeling and sailing to and from the reef in a Hobie Cat. If you come before 10:30 A.M., a 1.5-hour trip is US$28 per person. Or you can rent snorkel gear (US$5) and a kayak (US$10/20 single/double per hour) to create your own tour. Be sure to ask about a small anchor so your kayak doesn't float away, and lockers and dry bags for your stuff.

Wind Sports

Kiteboarding, sailboarding, and sailing have grown in popularity along the Caribbean, a trickle-down effect from the world-famous wind belt on the Gulf coast northwest of here. You can catch at least some breeze almost any time of the year, but the strongest, most consistent winds blow November–March.

Ikarus (5 Av. and Calle 20, tel. 984/803-3490, www.kiteboardmexico.com, 8:30 A.M.–9 P.M. daily) is a full-service kiteboarding retail shop and school. Classes are typically conducted at Isla Blanca, in the massive flat-water Chacmochuch Lagoon north of Cancún, which is ideal for kiting but nearly two hours by car or bus from Playa del Carmen. The shop doesn't include or arrange transport, nor is there lodging at Isla Blanca; many clients book here but stay in Cancún. Private classes are US$75 an hour or US$350 for six hours, while groups are US$55 an hour per person (maximum three to a group) or US$270 for six hours. Equipment is included for students, or can be rented separately (US$60 half day, US$90 full day). A sister store is two blocks south at Quinta Avenida and Calle 16.

Jaime's Marina (Playa El Faro, end of Calle 10, tel. 984/130-2034, www.jaimesmarina.bravehost.com, 9 A.M.–5 P.M. daily) offers

sailing classes and rentals from its kiosk on Playa El Faro. A four-hour beginner's class is US$130 for up to four people. Rent a three-person Hobie Cat for US$35–45 an hour (depending on how long you stay out), or a five-seater for US$45–75 an hour, with or without a guide.

Swimming with Dolphins

With swimming pens set up in the ocean, **Delphinus Riviera Maya** (Hwy. 307 Km. 282, toll-free Mcx. tel. 800/335-3461, www.delphinus.com.mx, US$159–499) is about as good as it gets for performing dolphins. For visitors, it's one of the most rewarding dolphin interaction programs in the region. For US$159, participants are permitted to interact with a dolphin pod for 50 minutes; standard tricks are performed while visitors are in the water—a series of jumps, a foot push, and a dolphin kiss—along with extras like just plain swimming with the pod. For US$499, a similar program is offered one-on-one with a dolphin. Ticket prices include a locker, towel, goggles, and round-trip transportation from many of the hotels on the Riviera Maya. There's a 10 percent discount if you book online.

Sport Fishing

Playa de Carmen has excellent sport and bottom fishing, with plentiful wahoo, *dorado,* mackerel, snapper, barracuda, and—especially April–June—sailfish and marlin. On average, trips for 1–5 people last 4–5 hours and cost US$200, including tackle and drinks. Most dive shops offer tours, as does Jaime's Marina (Playa El Faro, end of Calle 10, tel. 984/130-2034, www.jaimesmarina.bravehost.com, 9 A.M.–5 P.M. daily).

Golf

The **Golf Club at Playacar** (Paseo Xaman-Há opposite Hotel Viva Azteca, tel. 998/881-6088, www.palaceresorts.com, 6 A.M.–6 P.M. daily) is a challenging 7,144-yard championship course designed by Robert Van Hagge and located in Playacar, the upscale hotel and residential development south of Playa del Carmen proper.

Green fees are US$190 adult, US$130 after 2 P.M., and US$70 for children under age 17 (accompanied by adult), including cart, snacks, and drinks; free hotel pickup is included for full-price rounds. Reserve at least a day in advance November–January.

Ecotours

Alltournative (5 Av. btwn. Calles 12 and 14, tel. 984/803-9999, toll-free U.S./Canada tel. 800/507-1092, www.alltournative.com, 9 A.M.–7 P.M. daily, US$89–119 adult, US$82–95 child under 12) offers fun daily tours that include activities such as kayaking, zip lines, off-road bicycling, caving, and snorkeling, plus (depending on the tour you choose) visits to a small Maya village and Cobá archaeological zone. There are guides who speak English, Italian, French, German, Dutch, and Spanish. There's a second office in front of the bus station (5 Av. btwn. Calles 2 and 4).

Skydiving and Scenic Flights

Gleaming white beaches and brilliant turquoise seas make the Riviera Maya a spectacular place for skydiving. If you're up for it, **Sky Dive Playa** (Plaza Marina, tel. 984/873-0192, www.skydive.com.mx, 9 A.M.–sunset daily) has been throwing travelers out of planes at 10,000 feet since 1996. You freefall for 4,500 feet—about 45 seconds—then the 'chute opens for a 7-to-8-minute ride down to a soft landing on the beach. Tandem dives (you and an instructor, US$229) are offered every day—reserve 1–2 days in advance in summer and high season.

If you enjoy the view but prefer to stay buckled in, **Alas Sky Tour** (Playa del Carmen Airport, tel. 984/803-3718, www.mexcon.net/alas.htm, 9 A.M.–sunset Mon.–Sat., US$99 single, US$149 double) offers 25-minute scenic tours in a piloted ultralight aircraft. Sunset flights are gorgeous but can be bouncy.

Aerosaab (20 Av. Sur near Calle 1, tel. 984/873-0804, www.aerosaab.com) offers scenic full-day tours throughout the region—Chichén Itzá, Isla Holbox, Mérida, Uxmal—and

as far as Palenque. Trips are in 4- or 5-seat Cessna airplanes and run US$230–450 per person, plus airport fees. Most trips require a minimum of two people.

Spas and Gyms

Playa's swankiest gym is **Area Body Zone** (Paseo del Carmen, south end of 10 Av., www.areabodyzone.com, 6 A.M.–11 P.M. Mon.–Thurs., 6 A.M.–10 P.M. Fri., 7 A.M.–5 P.M. Sat.–Sun.), with the latest exercise machines, spacious free-weight and weight-machine areas, and regular sessions of aerobics, spinning, Pilates, and yoga. Day visits cost US$15, a 10-visit package US$55, and a month's membership US$110.

Across the street from the Shangri La Caribe, **El Jardín de los Aluxes** (Calle 38 at Calle Flamingo, 7:30 A.M.–9 P.M. Mon.–Fri., 8 A.M.–9 P.M. Sat., US$8 per class, US$50 per month) is an undeveloped jungly space reserved for, among others things, yoga instruction, tai chi classes, and spiritual growth seminars. Instruction is mostly held in a huge *palapa* but students are free to wander (and practice) on the lush property.

The well-tended **Unidad Deportiva Villanueva Madrid** (10 Av. near Calle 30, 6 A.M.–10:30 P.M. daily) is Playa del Carmen's public sporting facility with a gym, tennis and basketball courts, track, and soccer field. All have night lighting and are open to the public at no charge; BYO equipment.

Treat yourself to an afternoon of pampering at **Spa Itzá** (Calle Corazón at 5 Av., tel. 984/803-2588, www.spaitza.com, 8 A.M.–10 P.M. daily), a full-service spa in the heart of Playa. Massage therapies (US$45–110), Maya healing baths (US$55), body treatments (US$55–95), and facials (US$70–110) are among the rejuvenating services offered.

ACCOMMODATIONS

Playa del Carmen has a huge selection and variety of accommodations, from youth hostels to swanky resorts to condos and long-term rentals. Most all-inclusives are located in Playacar, just south of town.

Under US$25

◖ Youth Hostel Playa (Calle 8 near 25 Av., tel. 984/803-3277, www.hostelplaya.com, US$13.50 dorm, US$43 s/d with shared bath) is Playa del Carmen's best hostel, despite being somewhat removed from downtown and the beach. The dorm rooms are narrow but clean, and have thick, comfortable mattresses, individual fans, and free lockers. The private rooms are kept very clean, although light sleepers may be bothered by street noise. A well-equipped kitchen has plenty of space to work your culinary magic and a good cubby system to prevent groceries from disappearing. Best of all is the hostel's enormous common area, perfect for eating, playing cards, reading, watching TV, or whatever.

Urban Hostel (10 Av. btwn. Calles 4 and 6, tel. 984/803-3378, www.urbanhostel. mx, US$12 dorm, US$30 s/d with shared bath) has a welcoming entrance but the charm dries up somewhere in the narrow tunnel-like hallway that leads to the dorms and common area. Even a renovation didn't manage to improve the grubby, claustrophobic feeling here. Easy access to the bus terminal, free bike rental, and the cheapest rates in town (by a hair) are reason enough for some to stay, but there are better budget options to be had.

El Palomar Hostel (5 Av. btwn. Av. Juárez and Calle 2, tel. 984/873-0144, www.elpalomarhostel.com, US$12 dorm, US$38 s/d) has giant dorm rooms crammed with row upon row of double bunks, and three smallish private rooms with a clean, shared bathroom and a terrace with hammocks and a view of the ocean. The problem is there's no common area, save the rooftop terrace with an open-air kitchen. The hostel is right across from the bus terminal; Internet access, continental breakfast, and large lockers are included.

US$25-50

Near the bus station and with private access to a nice stretch of beach, **Cabañas Popol-Vuh** (Calle 2 near 5 Av., tel. 984/803-2149, pdcpopul_vuh@hotmail.com, US$20 s/d *cabañas* with shared bath, US$30 s/d *cabaña*

with private bath, US$54 s/d with private bath and a/c) has nine cozy *cabañas* and three hotel rooms facing a small sand lot. The *cabañas* are simple wood-paneled structures but they're comfortable enough, with good screens and strong fans. The only downer is the shared bathrooms, which need a serious scrub down—wear your flip-flops. The hotel rooms are a step up from the rest: tile floors, cable TV, mini-air-conditioners, and a private bathroom. In this town, these units are a steal—and go fast. Call ahead to reserve.

US$50-100

Hotel Casa Tucán (Calle 4 btwn. 10 and 15 Avs., tel. 984/873-0283, www.casatucan.de, US$50–60 s/d, US$70 studio) offers a labyrinth of basic rooms in a social environment. There are rustic *cabañas* with reasonably clean bathrooms, no-frill hotel rooms with fans, and small studios with even smaller kitchenettes. All of the units have fantastic murals, which spruce up the place. The hotel also boasts one of the deepest pools around at 4.8 meters (15.7 ft.). (It's so deep, in fact, that it's used by dive shops for open-water certification training.) Surrounded by lounge chairs and hammocks, it's perfect for whiling away an afternoon. Wireless Internet is also available.

◖ Hotel Casa de las Flores (20 Av. btwn. Calles 4 and 6, tel. 984/873-2898, www.hotelcasadelasflores.com, US$80–90 s/d with a/c) offers a cheerful hacienda-esque exterior that gives way to a leafy courtyard and garden, with a small stone-paved pool and rooms arranged on two levels in back. Americans will appreciate the air-conditioning, Europeans the bidet, and no one can complain about the simple but classy decor. Higher-priced rooms are bigger and have better light or small terraces, plus a mini-fridge.

Hotel Barrio Latino (Calle 4 btwn. 10 and 15 Avs., tel. 984/873-2384, www.hotelbarriolatino.com, US$60–80 s/d with a/c) offers charming rooms with mosaic-tile bathrooms, stone-inlaid floors, and private balconies. A complimentary continental breakfast is served in a leafy courtyard with a *palapa-*

roofed lounge—a good place to write postcards or play cards. Wireless Internet access and most international phone calls are also included in the rate. Somewhat uppity service is the only complaint.

Hotel LunaSol (Calle 4 btwn. 15 and 20 Avs., tel. 984/873-3933, www.lunasolhotel.com, US$94 s/d with fan, US$104 s/d with a/c) offers 16 comfortable rooms, all with private balconies or terraces, that are spread out between two modern thatch-roofed buildings. The spotless rooms have nice tile bathrooms, mini-fridges, and flat-screen TVs. Ask for one on the 2nd floor—those have high ceilings and the best cross breezes. Best of all, there's a fully equipped outdoor kitchen for guest use as well as a refreshing swimming pool with hot tub in the back garden.

Luna Blue Hotel & Garden (Calle 26 btwn. 5 and 10 Avs., tel. 984/873-0990, www.lunabluehotel.com, US$78–112 s/d with a/c) is a leafy oasis, and excellent value, just off busy Quinta Avenida. Rooms are tidy, if a bit sterile, and range from standards to suites with kitchen to top-floor Treetop Terrace units with sunny private balconies. Most have views of the garden, with its colorful Adirondack chairs under a canopy of tropical trees. A friendly bar, wireless Internet, beach club passes, and purified water are all included.

Located at a peaceful section of Quinta Avenida, **Hotel La Riviera** (5 Av. btwn. Calles 22 and 24, tel. 984/873-3240, www.hotellariviera.com, US$65–75 s/d with a/c) is agreeable and affordable, with clean no-frills rooms, all with sponge-painted walls, tile bathrooms, cable TV, and quiet air-conditioners. Rooms in front have balconies that overlook Quinta Avenida, which makes for more noise but is also a great people-watching spot. Wireless Internet is accessible to all guests and a decent Italian restaurant is on the ground floor.

US$100-150

Playa Maya (on the beach btwn. Calles 6 and 8, tel. 984/803-2022, www.playa-maya.com, US$135–185 s/d with a/c) is one of relatively few small hotels in Playa that have direct beach

access—a great feature. All 20 rooms are modern and comfortable, including some with kitchen, balcony, and ocean views. The beach is somewhat rocky right at the waterline, but still attractive and relaxing, and the hotel has lounge chairs and shaded tables right on the sand. But the beach entrance has its drawbacks, too—you may end up lugging your bags across the sand if there's no porter around to help.

Hotel Riviera Caribe Maya (10 Av. at Calle 30, tel. 984/873-1193, www.hotelrivieramaya.com, US$90–170 s/d with a/c) offers bright rooms with hand-carved Mexican furnishings and modern amenities like mini-air-conditioners, cable TV, in-room phone, and mini-fridge. Many have patios or balconies that look out onto the hotel's small inviting pool, which is tucked into a pleasant courtyard. Wireless Internet access and continental breakfast are included in the rate.

On a shady street just half a block from the beach, ◼ **Acanto Hotel and Suites** (Calle 16 near 5 Av., tel. 984/873-1252, www.acantohotels.com, US$125–265 suite with kitchen and a/c) has seven lovely one-bedroom condominiums with rich South Asian decor. Each has a fully equipped kitchen, a living-dining room, and patio, and is decorated in dark woods, luxurious fabrics, and fine art. A small swimming pool with a large Buddha to one side sits in the middle of the complex; there's a sundeck for guests who want to take in the sun without leaving the premises. Acanto also has larger deluxe condos for rent in a nearby complex.

The front and back sections at **Aventura Mexicana Hotel** (Calle 24 btwn. 5 and 10 Avs., tel. 984/873-1876, www.aventuramexicanahotel.com, US$140–200 with a/c) are priced the same, but are like two different hotels in terms of quality. The boutique-inspired back rooms have muted colors, elegant furnishings, and high-end amenities, and open onto a nicely manicured garden and peaceful pool—2nd floor units are even better, as there's less foot traffic. By contrast, the front rooms have plain decor and furnishings, and a nondescript pool in the center. A continental breakfast is included.

US$150-200

(The Blue Pearl Suites (1 Av. btwn. Calles 10 and 12, tel. 984/803-2379, www.thebluepearl.com.mx, US$160 s/d with a/c) offers stylish, comfortable, and ecofriendly apartments that typically sleep two to four people but have room for up to eight. All have fully equipped kitchens (complete with recycling and composting bins) and a private balcony or patio with hammocks and an outdoor tub. Rooms have gorgeous original art but otherwise pleasingly minimalist decor, plus wireless Internet and daily cleaning (even your dishes!). Guests have free access to Coco Maya beach club a short distance away, and there's a nice public beach around the corner; spa passes are also available. A small rooftop pool and lounge area are nice for enjoying the sun and impressive view. Be aware that some units have steep spiral staircases, and noise from nearby bars may disrupt light sleepers, especially on weekends (the a/c units help mask the din, however).

Over US$200

Removed from town and fronting on one of the best beaches in Playa, **(Hotel Las Palapas** (Calle 34 btwn. 5 Av. and the beach, tel. 984/873-4260, www.laspalapas.com, US$176–235 s, US$206–276 d) offers 75 rooms in one- and two-story thatched-roof bungalows, opening onto either a lush garden brimming with native flora or a white-sand beach with breathtaking views. All *cabañas,* as they're referred to here, are peaceful, with comfortable beds, ample patios with hammocks, and radio access to an exceptional staff—no televisions or phones here. A stone-lined path leads guests to an inviting freshwater pool, a clubhouse, a full-service spa, a dive shop, and—of course—beach chairs and umbrellas on the Caribbean. Be sure to climb the tall lookout platform for a spectacular bird's-eye view of Playa del Carmen. Rates include a full buffet breakfast; half-board rates are available.

A sleek urban-chic hotel, **Deseo** (5 Av. at Calle 12, tel. 984/879-3620, www.hoteldeseo.com, US$199–255 s/d with a/c, US$278–311 suite with a/c) boasts rooms that look as if they belong in a modern art museum. Think bananas, flip-flops, and a bikini top hanging from the wall. Add minimalist furnishings, including a low-lying bed, streamlined fixtures, and photo-shoot lamps. Now, pump in some tunes—techno or modern bossa nova—and that's your room. Outside your door is the hotel's bar/lounge/pool area with queen-size mattresses serving as sun loungers, with flowing white curtains strung high above. Very cool. Unless, of course, you want to sleep—music from the lounge blasts until 2 A.M. The hotel provides earplugs—use 'em or join the party. A continental breakfast is included.

Just a block away, Deseo's hip younger sister, **Básico** (5 Av. near Calle 10, tel. 984/879-4448, www.hotelbasico.com, US$199–255 s/d with a/c, US$278–311 suite with a/c), has highend rooms with an industrial-warehouse style. Staffers say the inspiration comes from the oil tankers that ply the Gulf of Mexico. Needless to say, despite the stark, cement look, the rooms are ultraplush—deep beds, fine linens, flat-screen TVs, even Polaroid cameras. A retro seafood restaurant/lounge is on the top floor with views of the Caribbean. Like Deseo, it's ultracool and ultraloud: Techno will keep you up—or dancing—late into the night.

The ultramodern **Mosquito Blue** (5 Av. btwn. Calles 12 and 14, tel. 984/873-1245, toll-free Mex. tel. 800/999-6666, toll-free U.S. tel. 866/547-8756, toll-free Canada tel. 866/940-5518, www.mosquitoblue.com, US$220–320 s/d with a/c, US$300–510 suite) boasts lush interior courtyards with two amoeba-shaped pools, an impressive *palapa*-roofed lounge with comfy couches, and striking modern art throughout. Rooms, though somewhat cramped, are beautifully appointed and have high-end amenities: digital safes, wireless Internet, plush bathrobes, minibar, and cable TV. Its sister hotel, the aptly named **Mosquito Beach** (Calle 8 at the beach, tel. 984/873-0001) has similar rates and is located on a nice stretch of beach in the heart of town. No children under 17 are allowed on either property.

Facing a beautiful stretch of beach,

Shangri-La Caribe (Calle 38 near 5 Av., tel. 984/873-0611, www.shangrilacaribe.net, US$215–305 s, US$240–345 d, US$385 beachfront bungalow) is a 10-minute walk from town, but a world apart from the hubbub there. Over 100 *palapa*-roofed bungalows are connected by sand paths that lead to the resort's facilities: two swimming pools, three restaurants, two bars, an Internet center, and a dive shop. The bungalows are beginning to show their age but are comfortable nonetheless with private balcony or terrace. The hotel bars are often hopping, but this is also a place you can find a quiet nook and catch up on that novel you've been trying to finish. A full breakfast and dinner are included in the rate.

All-Inclusive Resorts

Most of Playa del Carmen's all-inclusives are in Playacar, an upscale hotel and residential development south of town.

Iberostar Tucan (Av. Xaman-Ha, tel. 984/877-2000, www.iberostar.com, US$320–450 d all inclusive) has a spacious lobby-entryway and wide attractive beach with palm trees, beach chairs, and mild surf. Separating the lobby and the beach is a broad patch of healthy, well-maintained coastal forest, where you can spot monkeys, parrots, and other native creatures in the treetops. After so many sterile and manicured resorts, this place feels like a welcome change of scenery. The pool is huge, and near the beach. Rooms occupy large buildings along the property's edges, and are clean and comfortable, though plain. Junior suites have sea views.

Riu Palace Riviera Maya (Av. Xaman-Ha, tel. 984/877-2290, www.riu.com, US$485–585 d all inclusive) is one of six all-inclusive Riu resorts clustered together in Playacar, and the most upscale, though each resort in the group has its own appeal. The Palace Riviera Maya has an Old World look, with a soaring marble-floored lobby, ornate iron work, and Renaissance-style paintings and artwork. The suite-only accommodations feature additional sitting areas, restrained colors and decor (unlike the gaudy mess common in so many all-inclusives), top-shelf liquors, and modern bathrooms, including hydro-massage tubs. The beach and pool areas are spacious and appealing, and there are well-supplied gym and spa areas. Nightlife here can be a bit sedentary—it's generally an older clientele—but the advantage of the Palace category is that you have access to the other Riu resorts, like the Tequila or Yucatán, which are often more lively.

Rental Properties

Playacar has scores of houses for rent of all sizes and styles. Prices vary considerably, but expect to pay a premium for ocean views and during peak seasons. A number of property-management companies rent houses, including **Playacar Vacation Rentals** (Calle 10 s/n, tel. 984/873-0418, toll-free U.S. tel. 866/862-7164, www.playacarvacationrentals.com) and **Vacation Rentals** (Plaza Antigua, Calle 10 s/n, tel. 984/873-2952, U.S. tel. 205/332-3458, www.playabeachrentals.com). Both offices are south of Avenida Juárez near the Playacar entrance.

FOOD

Playa del Carmen has scores of restaurants and eateries offering a variety of culinary delights. Walk a block or two down Quinta Avenida and you're sure to spot something that you like.

Mexican

La Cueva del Chango (Calle 38 at 5 Av., 984/116-3179, 8 A.M.–11 P.M. Mon.–Sat., 8 A.M.–2 P.M. Sun., US$5–15) means The Cave of the Monkey, but the restaurant is neither dim nor primitive: The covered dining area has light-hearted decor (and a back patio ensconced in leafy vegetation) while the menu features crepes, empanadas, and innovative items like eggs with polenta and *chaya*. Well north of town, it's often packed with Playa's upper crust, though the prices make it accessible to all.

An old-school Mexican coffee shop, **Café Andrade** (Calle 8 near 20 Av., tel. 998/846-8257, 7 A.M.–11 P.M. daily, US$2–5) serves up mean breakfast and dinner plates with tacos, *chilaquiles,* mole, enchiladas…you name it, they'll whip it up. It's so typical, in fact, that you're likely only to see locals—during the week, businessmen puffing away at cigarettes, on weekends, families out for a bite.

For regional *tortas* (sandwiches), check out **Tortas del Carmen** (15 Av. btwn. Calles 2 and 4, tel. 984/129-7157, 8:30 A.M.–9 P.M. Mon.–Fri., 10 A.M.–9 P.M. Sat., noon–9 P.M. Sun., US$3–4), serving massive sesame rolls piled high with refried beans, cabbage, avocado, *quesillo* (a soft cheese), tomatoes, and your choice of meat. Try the Del Carmen, with pulled pork and chicken-fried steak, to fill up after a day at the beach. Only outdoor seating is available.

Unassuming and refreshingly untouristy, **La Pesca** (30 Av. near Av. Constituyentes, no phone, noon–10 P.M. daily, US$3–15) specializes in super-fresh seafood, including hefty fish and shrimp plates, tasty ceviche, and great fish tacos. (*La pesca* means the catch.) It's a bit of a hike from the center and boasts a view of the Mega supermarket, but is a nice way to get off Quinta Avenida.

Other Specialties

John Gray's Kitchen (Calle Corazón near Calle 14, tel. 984/803-3689, 6–10 P.M. Mon.–Sat., US$10–20) is a sister restaurant to the original John Gray's Kitchen in Puerto Morelos, widely considered one of the best restaurants on the Riviera Maya. The new kid lives up to expectations, expertly fusing gourmet American cuisine with flavors from around the world. The menu changes daily, but expect dishes like asparagus soup or spicy crab cakes with cilantro-leek fondue, and entrées of roasted duck with tequila, chipotle and honey, or linguine with truffled shrimp. Credit cards are not accepted, so you may want to stop at the ATM before dinner. Don't worry, it's worth it.

The first inklings of Arabic culture came to Mexico with the Spanish colonizers, whose food and architecture were deeply influenced by the Moors. Then came a wave of Palestinian and Lebanese immigrants who settled here in the 18th and 19th centuries. (Mexican actress Salma Hayek is of Lebanese descent, in fact.) So it's no surprise to find a restaurant like **Maktub Caffé** (5 Av. btwn. Calles 28 and 30, 2 P.M.–midnight daily, US$5–12), which serves excellent tabbouleh, hummus, falafel, and hookahs and flavored tobacco to relax by. It's on a hip, bustling block, with restaurants and bars on both sides and across the street.

Friendly and unassuming, **Ula-Gula** (5 Av. at Calle 10, 2nd Fl., tel. 984/879-3727, 5:30–11:30 P.M. daily, US$9–25) serves outstanding international gourmet dinners in an appealing 2nd-floor dining area overlooking Quinta Avenida. Argentinean-owned and -operated, the pasta and meat dishes are excellent as expected, but seafood is the real standout here, whether appetizers like tuna with wasabi and soy sauce, or the fish of the day, prepared in unique fashion, like with a parsley gorgonzola sauce. For dessert, the chocolate fondant—a small chocolate cake filled with rich chocolate syrup and accompanied by ice cream—is divine.

Although occasionally missing the mark, old-timer **Babe's Noodles and Bar** (Calle 10 btwn. 5 Av. and 10 Av., tel. 984/804-1998, noon–11 P.M. Mon.–Sat., 5–11 P.M. Sun., US$6–14) still serves up delicious Thai and Asian-fusion meals in a hip bistro setting. Dishes come in half and full orders. Don't miss a chance at ordering the *limonmenta,* an awesome lime-mint slushie. It's not a huge place so you may have to wait for a table during high season, or if you prefer, head to its sister restaurant down the street (5 Av. btwn. Calles 28 and 30, 2–11 P.M. Mon.–Sat.). No credit cards are accepted.

Madre Tierra (5 Av. at Calle 14, tel. 984/803-0222, 1 P.M.–midnight daily, US$10–25) is a classy seafood and steak house with a prominent 2nd-floor location overlooking Quinta Avenida. (Playa buffs will remember this as Apasionado's former location.) The restaurant serves only imported certified Angus beef, from sirloin to ribs, plus fresh fish, lobster and shellfish, and a variety of salads, pastas, and desserts. A hostess stationed on street level entices passersby to enter with free drink tickets (especially if you waver a bit).

THE RIVIERA MAYA

100% Natural (5 Av. btwn. Calles 10 and 12, tel. 984/873-2242, 7 A.M.–11 P.M. daily, US$5–11) serves mostly vegetarian dishes and a large selection of fresh fruit blends. Service can be a bit inattentive here, but the food is fresh and well prepared. Tables are scattered through a leafy garden area and covered patio.

Better known as a wine bar, **Di Vino** (5 Av. at Calle 12, 7:30–11:30 A.M., 12:15 P.M.–midnight daily, US$8–18) also has excellent meals, including a large deluxe breakfast buffet for US$9. The lunch and dinner menu includes a mix of Mexican and international dishes, and of course wines of all sorts, served in a cool upscale setting.

Cafés and Bakeries

Chocolate lovers will melt over **Ah Cacao** (5 Av. at Av. Constituyentes, tel. 984/803-5748, www.ahcacao.com, 7:15 A.M.–11:45 P.M. daily, US$1.50–4.50), a chocolate café where every item on the menu—from coffees to cakes—is homemade from the finest of beans. Try a spicy Maya Chocolate for a true taste treat (US$3). A sister shop (Calle 30 near 5 Av., tel. 984/879-4179) is located up the street from Playa Mamitas.

Next door to Ah Cacao is a treat of another kind—real bagels in Mexico! **Karma Bagels** (5 Av. btwn. Av. Constituyentes and Calle 20, 11 A.M.–midnight daily, US$3–7) serves up creative sandwiches on fresh-made bagels—the Master of the Skies includes chicken breast, spinach á la crème, and goat cheese—along with tasty salads. The airy 2nd-floor dining area overlooks a busy roundabout, and makes for good people-watching.

You'll smell **C Hot** (Calle Corazón at Calle 14, 7:30 A.M.–10 P.M. daily, US$2–8) from a block away—this café bakes fresh breads and pastries all day. Most people end up staying for more than just a brownie though—the full menu of sandwiches prepared on whole-wheat or sunflower-seed bread is almost impossible to resist. The shady outdoor eating area is a great place to enjoy a leisurely breakfast, too.

The charming Old World **C Café Sasta** (5 Av. btwn. Calles 8 and 10, 7 A.M.–11 P.M.

daily, US$1.50–4.50) offers a tempting display of muffins, scones, cupcakes—even cheese-cake—to go along with the full coffee menu. Seating is available indoors and outdoors.

Service can be slow, but **Café Corazón** (5 Av. btwn. Calles 28 and 30, no phone, 7:30 A.M.–midnight daily, US$4–10) is a place to enjoy the wait, with Italian coffee and fresh-squeezed juice, and pleasant outdoor tables. Sandwiches figure prominently on the menu, with fillers like smoked salmon, Italian salami, avocado, and egg, served on a baguette, bagel, or toast.

Groceries

Wal-Mart (Calle 8 btwn. Avs. 20 and 25, 7 A.M.–midnight daily) has arrived in Playa, opening a huge superstore right behind city hall—how's that for a metaphor?—with ev-erything from clothes, shoes, and snorkel gear to groceries, prepared food, and a full pharmacy.

INFORMATION AND SERVICES
Tourist Information

Playa's tourist information (Av. Juárez at Calle 15, tel. 984/873-2804, 9 A.M.–9 P.M. Mon.–Fri., 9 A.M.–5 P.M. Sat.–Sun.) is well stocked with brochures and maps. You may also find copies of *La Quinta* or *Sac-Be,* free monthly magazines that usually offer a handful of use-ful articles, listings, and events calendars.

Emergency Services

Hospiten Riviera Maya (main highway, tel. 984/803-1002, www.hospiten.com, 24 hours) is a private hospital offering modern, high-quality medical service at reasonable rates. Many of the doctors have U.S. training and speak English, and are accustomed to treating foreign visitors and expats. Playa also has a hyperbaric cham-ber, operated by **Playa International Clinic** (10 Av. at Calle 28 Norte, tel. 984/803-1215, emergency tel. 984/873-1365, 9 A.M.–8 P.M. Mon.–Fri., 9 A.M.–2 P.M. and 5–8 P.M. Sat.–Sun.). For emergency ambulance service, call 065 from any public phone. **Farmacia Yza** (tel. 984/873-2727) is a 24-hour pharmacy located on 10 Avenida between Calles 12 and 14; order at least US$10 of medicine or snacks (it's also a mini-mart) and they'll deliver to your hotel. The **tourist police** (tel. 984/877-3340, or 060 from any pay phone) have an office on Avenida Juárez and 15 Avenida, and informational kiosks along Quinta Avenida, theoretically operating 24 hours a day.

Money

Banamex (Calle 12 at 10 Av., 9 A.M.–4 P.M. Mon.–Fri., 10 A.M.–2 P.M. Sat.) and **Banorte** (Plaza Pelícanos, 10 Av. btwn. Calles 8 and 10, 9 A.M.–6 P.M. Mon.–Fri., 10 A.M.–2 P.M. Sat.) are full-service banks with ATMs and foreign exchange, or try the freestanding **cash machine** at the corner of Quinta Avenida and Calle 20, one of several around town.

Media and Communications

The **post office** (9 A.M.–4 P.M. Mon.–Fri., 9 A.M.–noon Sat.) is next to the tourist police office at the corner of Avenida Juárez and 15 Avenida. Postcards and small letters cost US$1 to send to the United States, US$1.35 to Europe.

There's no shortage of Internet cafés in Playa, most offering additional services like international phone calls, Skype, photo downloads, CD burning, and more. At the south end of town, try **Phonet Centro de Comunicaciones** (10 Av. btwn. Calles 2 and 4, 8 A.M.–11 P.M. daily, Internet US$1.50/hr) or **Cybernet** (Calle 8 btwn. 5 Av. and the beach, tel. 984/873-3476, 8 A.M.–11:30 P.M. daily). At the other end of Quinta Avenida is **PTIT Devil** (5 Av. at Calle 28, 8 A.M.–11 P.M. daily), where air-conditioning and armchairs make checking email cool and comfortable, and small outdoor tables with individual phones make calling equally pleasant. A few blocks away, **Centro de Comunicaciones 24** (5 Av. and Calle 20, 24 hours, Internet US$2.25/hr) is often filled with clouds of cigarette smoke, but it also never closes and offers 30 percent off international calling on weekends. It has a sister cybercafé on Calle 24 between Quinta Avenida and 1 Avenida Norte 24 (8 A.M.–midnight daily).

Immigration

Playa del Carmen's immigration office (Plaza Antigua mall, 2nd Fl., Calle 10, tel. 998/881-3560, 9 A.M.–1 P.M. Mon.–Fri.) is located on the road to Playacar. Avoid using it, however, as the one in Cancún is more efficient. A tourist visa extension, or *prórroga,* can take a week or more in Playa and involves considerable documentation; in Cancún, the same process is simplified and takes as little as two hours.

Laundry

A convenient place to get your threads washed is **Lavendería Premium Los Mecates** (Calle 4 near 20 Av., 8:30 A.M.–8 P.M. Mon.–Fri., 8:30 A.M.–1 P.M. Sat.–Sun., US$1/kilogram). Same-day service is available if you drop your clothes off early.

Language and Instruction

Playa del Carmen is becoming a popular place to study Spanish, with several schools, plenty of options for cultural and historical excursions, and of course good nightlife and great beaches.

Solexico (35 Av. btwn. Calles 6 and 6-Bis, tel. 984/873-0755, www.solexico.com) is a highly recommended school with a reputation for professionalism. Classes are offered in groups of no more than five people or individual classes, and for 15, 25, or 40 hours per week (US$161–619 per week). All levels of courses are offered, including instruction geared toward professionals who have regular contact with Spanish speakers. Students can stay with local families (US$175–196/ week with breakfast, US$196–224/week half board), at the school's 10-room student residence (US$210–266 per week including breakfast), or arrange for hotel and condo rentals. Ask about volunteer opportunities.

Playalingua del Caribe (Calle 20 btwn. 5 and 10 Av., tel. 984/873-3876, www.playalingua.com, 8 A.M.–8 P.M. daily) has a spacious learning center with a leafy garden and small private pool. Courses vary from standard to intensive classes (10 hours/week or 20–25 hours/

THE RIVIERA MAYA

PLAYA DEL CARMEN BUS SCHEDULES

Terminal Turística (5 Av. and Av. Juárez, tel. 984/873-0109, ext. 2501, toll-free Mex. tel. 800/702-8000) is located near the ferry dock and has frequent service north to Cancún and south to Tulum, and most locations in between. Long-distance buses use the Terminal Alterna.

Most Tulum-bound buses stop at the turnoffs for destinations along the way, including **Xcaret** (US$1.25, 10 mins), **Paamul** (US$1.25, 15 mins), **Puerto Aventuras** (US$1.25, 20 mins), **Xpu-Há** (US$1.75, 25 mins), **Akumal** (US$2.25, 30 mins), **Xel-Ha** (US$3.50, 30 mins), and **Hidden Worlds** and **Dos Ojos** (both US$3.50, 40 mins).

Most Chetumal-bound buses stop at **Carrillo Puerto** (US$7.50-10, 2-2.5 hrs) and **Bacalar** (US$13, 4.5 hrs).

Most Cancún-bound buses stop at **Puerto Morelos** (US$1.70, 35 mins) but *not* the airport or Cancún's Zona Hotelera.

DESTINATION	PRICE	DURATION	SCHEDULE
Cancún	US$3.50	1 hr	every 10 mins 5:20 A.M.-midnight
Cancún Int'l Airport	US$8	1 hr	hourly 7 A.M.-7:15 P.M.
Chetumal (2nd class)	US$15	6 hrs	every 1-2 hrs 5:30 A.M.-5:30 P.M., plus 11:30 P.M. (making all stops)
Tulum	US$2-4	1-1.5 hrs	every 30-60 mins 5:30 A.M.-1:45 A.M.
Xcaret (main entrance)	US$3	15 mins	9 A.M., 9:40 A.M., 10:20 A.M., 11 A.M., 11:40 A.M.

week) and are offered in 4–6 person groups, two-person workshops, or one-on-one settings. Rates vary accordingly, from US$110 to US$320 per week. Lodging options include staying with a local family (US$180/week half-board), in a shared or private apartment (US$30–100/day), or in small, clean, air-conditioned rooms right at the school, so you can roll out of bed and be conjugating verbs in a matter of minutes (US$175–265 pp/week, including breakfast). One-time materials and inscription fees are about US$110; weekend excursions and extras classes, including Maya language, Mexican cooking, and wood and stone carving, are also available.

International House (Calle 14 Norte btwn. 5 Av. and 10 Av., tel. 984/803-3388, www.ihrivieramaya.com, 7:30 A.M.–9 P.M. Mon.–Fri., 7:30 A.M.–noon Sat.) occupies a pretty and peaceful colonial home, with a large classroom, garden, bar, and restaurant on-site. All instructors are university graduates with training in teaching Spanish as a foreign language. Group classes meet for four hours per day Monday to Friday, and have a maximum of eight students, though typically just 3–4 (US$220/week, free enrollment and materials, ages 16 and over only). Private and two-person classes are also available (US$30–35/ hour), as are custom courses for medical professionals, teachers, and other groups, plus additional activities like diving, Mexican cooking,

Terminal Alterna (Calle 20 btwn. Calles 12 and 12-Bis, tel. 984/803-0944, toll-free Mex. tel. 800/702-8000) departures include:

DESTINATION	PRICE	DURATION	SCHEDULE
Campeche	US$38	8 hrs	10:30 A.M.
Chetumal	US$19-23	5 hrs	every 1-2 hrs 6:15 A.M.-11:55 P.M.
Chichén Itzá	US$19	4 hrs	8 A.M.
Cobá	US$7	2 hrs	8 A.M.
Mérida	US$28-33	5.5 hrs	every 1-2 hrs 6:15 A.M.-6:30 P.M., plus 10:30 P.M., 11:30 P.M., and midnight
Palenque	US$48-57	12 hrs	Take San Cristóbal bus
San Cristóbal (Chiapas)	US$62-72	19 hrs	3:30 P.M., 5 P.M., and 7 P.M.
Valladolid	US$13	2.5 hrs	7:30 A.M., 8 A.M., 10:20 A.M., 11:30 A.M., 2:30 P.M., 6:30 P.M., and 12:30 A.M.
Xpujil	US$26	5.5 hrs	9:50 A.M., 12:15 P.M., 3:35 P.M., 3:40 P.M., and 6:15 P.M.

THE RIVIERA MAYA

and Latin dancing. Family stays can be arranged for US$210–245 per week, with breakfast or half board, while a variety of furnished apartments and student rooms, single and shared, with or without meals, run US$140–335 per week.

GETTING THERE
Air
Playa del Carmen has an airport a few blocks from the ferry pier, but it's used for private and charter flights only, with just one runway and no official terminal. Commercial service is available at Cancún's international airport, a short drive north of Playa del Carmen.

Bus
Playa del Carmen has two bus stations: **Terminal Turística** (aka Terminal Riviera, 5 Av. and Av. Juárez) is in the center of town and has frequent second-class service to destinations along the coast, including Cancún, Tulum, and everything in between; **Terminal Alterna** (Calle 20 btwn. Calles 12 and 12 Bis) has first-class and deluxe service to interior destinations such as Mérida, Campeche, and beyond. There is some overlap, and you can buy tickets for any destination at either station, so always double-check from which station your bus departs.

Combi

Combis (shuttle vans, tel. 984/873-0032) are an easy way to get up and down the Riviera Maya. In Playa, northbound *combis* line up on Calle 2 near 20 Avenida, leaving every 15 minutes, from 3 A.M. to 1 A.M. daily. The final destination is Cancún's main bus terminal (US$3, 50 mins), but you can be dropped off anywhere along the highway, including Puerto Morelos (US$2, 20 mins). *Combis* do not enter Cancún's Zona Hotelera, but you can catch a bus there from outside the terminal.

South from Playa del Carmen, *combis* leave from the same corner every 15 minutes, 5 A.M.–10 P.M. daily. They go as far as the Tulum bus station (US$2.50, 1 hr), passing the turnoffs for Puerto Aventuras (US$2, 10 mins), Xpu-Há (US$2, 20 mins), Akumal (US$2, 25 mins), Hidden Worlds (US$2.50, 40 mins), Tankah Tres (US$2.50, 45 mins), and Tulum Ruins (US$2.50, 50 mins). To return, flag down a *combi* anywhere along the highway.

Come here to catch a ferry to Isla Cozumel.

Car

If you are driving to Playa del Carmen, look for the two main access roads to the beach—Avenida Constituyentes on the north end of town and Avenida Benito Juárez on the south. Playacar has its own entrance from the highway, but can also be reached by turning south on Calle 10 off Avenida Juárez.

Ferry

Passenger ferries to Cozumel (US$11 each way, 30 mins) leave from the pier at the end of Calle 1 Sur. **UltraMar** and **Mexico Water Jets** alternate departures and charge the same amount, though UltraMar's boats are newer. Their ticket booths are side by side at the foot of the pier, with the time of the next departure displayed prominently. The ticket seller will probably try to sell you a round-trip ticket, but it makes more sense, and costs the same, to buy a *sencilla* (one-way ticket) and wait to see which ferry has the next departure when you're ready to return. Between the two companies, there are ferries every hour 6 A.M.–10 P.M. daily.

Car ferries operated by **Transcaribe** (tel. 987/872-7688 in Cozumel) depart from the Calica/Punta Venado dock south of Playa at 1:30 P.M. and 6 P.M. Monday to Saturday (earlier departures are for freight only) and at 6 A.M. and 6 P.M. on Sunday. Returning from Cozumel, the ferry leaves from the international pier at 6 A.M., 11 A.M., 4 P.M., and 8:30 P.M. Monday to Saturday and at 8 A.M. and 8 P.M. on Sunday. The trip takes about 1.25 hours and costs US$45 for a car including driver, and US$5 for each additional passenger. Arrive at least an hour in advance to get a spot.

GETTING AROUND

Playa del Carmen is a walking town, although the steady northward expansion is challenging that description. The commercial part of Quinta Avenida now stretches 32 blocks and keeps getting longer. Cabs and bicycle taxis are a good option, especially if you have luggage.

Taxi

Taxis around town cost US$1.75–5, or a bit

more if you use a taxi stand or have your hotel summon one. All taxi drivers carry a *tarifario*—an official fare schedule—which you can ask to see if you think you're getting taken for a ride, so to speak. Prices do change every year or two, so ask at your hotel what the current rate is, and always be sure to agree on the fare with the driver before setting off.

Triciclos (bike-taxis) line up on Avenida Juárez alongside the Terminal Turística. The ride costs about the same as one in a taxi but makes an interesting open-air alternative.

Car

Playa has myriad car rental agencies and prices can vary considerably. Prices are highest at the major agencies, like Hertz, National, Avis, and Executive, but they often have great deals online. At local agencies, like **Veloz Rent a Car** (Av. Constituyentes btwn. 5 Av. and 1 Av. Norte, tel. 984/803-2323, 8 A.M.–1 P.M. and 5–8 P.M. daily) and **Zipp Rent-A-Car** (10 Av. btwn. Calles 2 and 4, tel. 998/873-0696, www.zipp.com.mx, 8 A.M.–6 P.M. daily), you

may be able to negotiate lower rates, especially during low season and for rentals of a week or more. Expect to pay US$45–60 a day for a car, with taxes and insurance included.

Parking in Playa in the high season can be a challenge, especially south of Avenida Constituyentes. Many hotels have secure parking; there are also parking lots around town, including on Calle 2 at 10 Avenida (8 A.M.–10 P.M. daily, US$1/hr or US$8.50/day).

PAAMUL

What started out as an unassuming trailer park on a beautiful stretch of beach has now become a seaside community all its own. Located about 20 kilometers (12.4 miles) south of Playa del Carmen, Paamul has everything from RVs with elaborate wood and *palapa* structures over them to hotel rooms, a restaurant, and even a dive shop.

Beach

Paamul stretches over a wide curving beach. It's clean and classically pretty with white sand and

Paamul is one of several hideaways along the Riviera Maya.

© LIZA PRADO

THE RIVIERA MAYA

turquoise water—perfect for swimming and exploring. Watch your step on the south end of the beach, as its waters harbor prickly sea urchin—consider wearing water shoes.

Snorkeling and Scuba Diving

Scuba-Mex (tel. 984/875-1066, toll-free U.S. tel. 888/871-6255, www.scubamex.com, 8 A.M.–5 P.M. daily) is a full-service shop offering one- and two-tank dive trips to open-water sites and cenotes (US$39–80 including equipment). A variety of packages and dive courses are available at competitive rates. If you're just interested in snorkeling off the beach, the shop rents snorkel gear for US$6 per day.

Accommodations

Offering a little bit of everything, **☾ Hotel Paa Mul** (Carr. Cancún–Chetumal Km. 85, tel. 999/925-9422, www.paamul.com, US$10 pp tent, US$25 RVs, US$115 s/d *cabañas,* US$150 s/d with a/c) appeals to travelers of all budgets. Best of all are the hotel rooms, which were built in 2006. All are boutique-y in style, with muted colors, luxurious linens, gleaming bathtubs, mini-air-conditioners, and gorgeous ocean views from private terraces. Next best are, surprisingly, the tent and trailer spaces. Although set up in the main parking lot, all

have electricity, running water, and clean shared hot-water bathrooms just steps from the Caribbean. Dead last are the *cabañas.* Constructed in 2000, they look as if they've been through decades of wear and tear: wood floors with holes, cement walls with paint thrown on, and granny-style decor. You're better off in a tent space.

Food

Open-air, modern, and with a great view of the Caribbean, the **Reefs of Paamul Restaurant and Bar** (8 A.M.–9 P.M. daily, US$5–16) serves up classic Mexican dishes along with a variety of international meals. There's something for everyone, which makes it easy to eat most of your meals here. (Good thing, since it's the only restaurant in Paamul).

For groceries, the very mini **Mini Super Paa Mul** (7 A.M.–7 P.M. Mon.–Sat., 8 A.M.–2 P.M. Sun.) sells basic foodstuffs. It's located at the highway turnoff to Paamul.

Information and Services

There are no health, banking, Internet, or postal services in Paamul. The closest town—and one of the best places in the region—for a full range of services is Playa del Carmen, 20 kilometers (12.4 miles) north.

Puerto Aventuras

Puerto Aventuras is an odd conglomeration of condos, summer homes, and hotels, organized around a large marina, including a swim-with-dolphins area. It's more than a resort, but not really a town. Whatever you call it, Puerto Aventuras's huge signs and gated entrance are impossible to miss, located a few minutes north of Akumal on Hwy. 307.

MUSEO SUB-ACUÁTICO CEDAM

Short for Conservation, Ecology, Diving, Archaeology, and Museums, CEDAM runs this very worthwhile museum (Bldg. F,

9 A.M.–1 P.M. and 2:30–5:30 P.M. Mon.–Sat., donation requested), displaying a wide variety of items: Maya offerings that were dredged from the peninsula's cenotes, artifacts recovered from nearby colonial shipwrecks, early diving equipment, and photos of open-water and cenote explorations, some from the halcyon days of diving when *jeans* were the preferred get-up.

SPORTS AND RECREATION

Snorkeling and Scuba Diving

Some 25 dive sites lie within a 10-minute boat ride from the marina, each boasting the rich

CEDAM AND THE RIVIERA MAYA

In 1948, a small group of Mexican divers – active frogmen during World War II – created a nonprofit organization called Club de Exploración y Deporte Acuáticos de México (Exploration and Aquatic Sports Club of Mexico, or CEDAM). Their mission was to promote ocean conservation and educate others about its treasures and resources.

In 1958, the group set about salvaging the *Mantanceros*, a Spanish galleon that foundered offshore in 1741. It got permission to set up camp in present-day Akumal, then just a deserted beach owned by a man named Argimiro Arguelles. Arguelles leased CEDAM a workboat for their project, and even offered his services as captain.

It was this relationship that sealed Akumal's – and arguably, the Riviera Maya's – destiny. During a relaxed evening around the campfire, Arguelles sold Pablo Bush, the head of CEDAM, the bay of Akumal and thousands of acres of coconut palms north and south of it. For the next 12 years, CEDAM continued its work in the rustic and beautiful place – replacing their tents with sturdy *palapa* huts, and still using the creaky SS *Cozumel* to carry divers to work sites up and down the coast.

It wasn't long before the idea of promoting tourism on Mexico's forgotten Caribbean coast arose. In 1968, the group – which had changed the words behind its initials to Conservation, Ecology, Diving, Archaeology, and Museums – donated 5,000 acres of land to the government, as well as the Cove of Xel-há, to create a national park. The aim was to open the isolated area to tourists, and in so doing, create jobs for local residents. CEDAM also provided housing, food, electricity, running water, a school for the children, and a first-aid station with a trained nurse.

Still based in Akumal, CEDAM has grown into an important international scientific and conservation organization. The group plays an active part in the archaeological exploration of cenotes, among other things, and hosts regular symposiums and seminars. A small but worthwhile museum in Puerto Aventuras – Museo Sub-Acuático CEDAM (Bldg. F, 9 A.M.-2 P.M. and 3:30-6 P.M. Mon.-Sat., donation requested) – displays some of the incredible items that the group has recovered in the region's waters.

coral, abundant sealife, and interesting features, like pillars and swim-throughs, found up and down the coast. **Aquanauts** (tel. 984/873-5041, toll-free U.S. tel. 877/623-2491, www.aquanauts-online.com, 8 A.M.–6 P.M. daily) is a safe full-service shop that has many repeat guests. Divers can count on personal details (such as storing dry gear) and guest-first practices (such as staying under as long as your air permits, not just the standard 45 minutes). The shop offers the full range of dives and courses, including reef dives (US$45/one tank, US$80/two tanks), cenote dives (US$125/two tanks) and certification courses, including open water (US$470 private, US$425 pp group). Multi-dive packages are available; equipment rental is included in courses but not fun dives (US$20/day). The shop also offers snorkel tours to the reef, cenotes, or a combination of both, or even a stop at Tulum ruins (US$45–90, including equipment, snacks, and drinks). Reservations are recommended in high season for all tours and courses.

Swimming with Dolphins

Dolphin Discovery (Marina, tel. 984/873-5078, toll-free U.S. tel. 866/393-5158, toll-free Canada tel. 866/793-1905, www.dolphindiscovery.com, 9 A.M.–5 P.M. daily) offers several dolphin-encounter activities, ranging in price based on the amount and type of interaction you have. For the most contact, the Royal Swim program (US$149, 30 mins orientation, 30 mins in water) includes two dolphins per group of 10 people, with a chance to do a "dorsal tow," "foot push," and "kiss," plus some open swim time. The Swim Adventure (US$99) and Dolphin Encounter (US$69/59

THE RIVIERA MAYA

© LIZA PRADO

Swimming with dolphins is one of the most popular activities along the Riviera Maya.

adult/child) have somewhat less direct contact. The center also has manatee and sea-lion programs that can be taken in combo with dolphins. Programs start at 9 A.M., 11 A.M., 1 P.M., and 3 P.M. daily; free shuttle service is available to and from Playa del Carmen.

Sport Fishing

Capt. Rick's Sportfishing Center (past Omni Puerto Aventuras hotel, tel. 984/873-5195, toll-free Mex. tel. 800/719-6439, www.fishyucatan.com, office 8 A.M.–7 P.M. daily) offers customized fishing trips for groups and individuals. Trolling is the most popular, going for *dorado,* tuna, barracuda, sailfish, and even marlin. Bottom/drift fishing is also fun and targets "dinner fish" such as grouper, snapper, and yellowtail. You can also arrange time for visiting a deserted beach or Maya ruin, snorkeling on the reef, or just cruising by upscale homes and hotels. Choose from 10 different boats, ranging in length from 23 to 46 feet, with capacity for 2–12 anglers. Rates are for half day (US$275–575), three-quarter day (US$375–775), and full day

(US$475–950). For a special outing, ask about *Last Flight Out,* a 56-foot ocean yacht with room for 15 anglers that costs US$750–1,500 for half-day and full-day trips. Shared trips are US$95 per person for half day and US$190 for full day, and typically utilize a 31-foot boat for up to six fishermen. All prices include equipment, bait, soft drinks, and water; full-day trips also include lunch. There's good fishing year-round, but April–July are best for hooking into a billfish.

Sailing

Fat Cat (Puerto Aventuras Marina, tel. 984/876-3316, www.fatcatsail.com) is a spacious custom-designed catamaran used for day-long excursions (US$89/49 adult/child) that include sailing to secluded Xaac Cove, with a nice beach, good snorkeling, and a small Maya ruin nearby. You can also try "boom netting," in which you are pulled through the water behind the boat on a thick boom net.

Parasailing

Riviera Maya Adventures (past Omni Puerto

Aventuras hotel, tel. 984/873-5623, www.snubamexico.com, 8 A.M.–6 P.M. daily) offers single and tandem parasail trips (US$65 single, US$55 pp tandem, 9 A.M., 10 A.M., and 11 A.M.) several times daily. The flights last 10–12 minutes (although the whole excursion takes about an hour) and you reach up to 250 feet in the air. Others can accompany you on the boat for US$20 per person. The agency caters to cruise ship passengers, so advance reservations are a good idea.

Golf and Tennis

Puerto Aventuras Club de Golf (across from Bldg. B, tel. 984/873-5109, 7:30 A.M.–5:30 P.M. daily, last tee time 3 P.M.) offers a nine-hole, par-36 golf course right in town. The course, designed in 1991 by Tom Leman, is flat but has two par 5s over a total 2,961 yards (3,255 championship). Green fees include a golf cart and are US$88 including cart; US$79 after 1 P.M., US$58 at 3 P.M. (nine holes only). Two tennis courts are available for US$21 an hour. Golf club rentals cost US$27, tennis racquets run US$5. Reservations are usually required.

ACCOMMODATIONS

The road into town bumps right into **Omni Puerto Aventuras** (tel. 984/875-1950, www.omnihotels.com, US$319 s/d with a/c), a small upscale resort with the marina on one side and a fine, palm-shaded beach on the other. There are just 30 rooms, all spacious and attractive, with colorful regional decor and modern amenities. Best of all, every room has a private patio and hot tub; those with ocean views are especially lovely, though they cost a bit more. The resort's small size and low-key atmosphere makes it easy to meet other guests, and nighttime typically finds everyone around the hot tub beach bar overlooking the beach and ocean. Wireless Internet is available, though the US$15/day fee seems excessive. Significant discounts are available in the low season.

C Casa del Agua (Punta Matzoma 21, tel. 984/873-5184, www.casadelagua.com, US$1,755 s/d with a/c per three nights, US$2,457 house per three nights) is a beacon of class and charm amid the plastic commercialism of Puerto Aventuras. At the southern end of town, the hotel's four spacious suites—the bathrooms alone are bigger than some hotel rooms—all have king-size beds, air-conditioning and fan, and come with a hearty breakfast served on a common patio overlooking the bay. There is a small sunny pool and the beach is quiet and private, although rather steeply sloped. Guests are free to borrow kayaks and snorkeling gear, as well as the hotel's wireless Internet signal. Service is superb. There's a three-night minimum stay, whether renting part or all of the house (which sleeps eight). The resort accommodates children 12 and older only.

FOOD

Stroll around Puerto Aventuras' marina and dolphin enclosure and you'll pass pretty much every restaurant in town.

Café Olé International (Bldg. A, tel. 984/873-5125, 7 A.M.–10 P.M. daily, US$5–25) has something for everyone and every price range. It's best known for its filet mignon and homemade desserts.

If you're in the mood for a big salad or a pizza—thin, regular, or deep dish— try **Richard's Quarterdeck Steakhouse and Pizza** (Bldg. A, tel. 984/873-5086, 11 A.M.–10 P.M. daily, US$6–32). The place was opened in 1994 by a Chicago native; the food here is especially good if you're missing flavors from home.

Super Akumal (across from Omni Puerto Aventuras hotel, 7 A.M.–10 P.M. Mon.–Sat., until 8 P.M. Sun.) is the local market and has a little of everything, including water, chips, sunscreen, toiletries, and so on. Be aware that you can't buy alcohol before 10 A.M. or after 9 P.M. Monday to Saturday, nor after 2 P.M. on Sunday.

INFORMATION AND SERVICES
Emergency Services

There is one local pharmacy, **First Aid Pharmacy** (Bldg. A, tel. 984/873-5305 or 984/206-6189, 9 A.M.–9 P.M. daily, or by telephone 24 hours).

THE RIVIERA MAYA

Money

Puerto Aventuras doesn't have an actual bank yet, but there's a Banamex ATM next to Capt. Rick's fishing shop and a Santander ATM near the entrance of Museo CEDAM. Both are accessible 24 hours.

Media and Communications

The **post office** (10 A.M.–2 P.M. Mon., Wed., and Fri.) is in a large kiosk a short distance from the golf club entrance. The coffee and brownies are great at **Café-C@fé** (tel. 984/873-5728, www.cafecafe-pa.com, 8 A.M.–6 P.M. daily, closed on Sunday in low season), where you can get online for US$5/hr (including Wi-Fi) or for much less with a prepaid 5- or 10-hour package. International calls cost US$0.40 to the United States and Canada, US$0.80 to the rest of the world. **Azul Tequila** (tel. 984/873-5673, 11 A.M.–11 P.M. Tues.–Sun.) is a small friendly restaurant-bar with Internet access for US$5 per hour, or for free if you order a drink or something to eat.

Laundry

Opposite the post office, **Mikamale Mami** (8 A.M.–10 P.M. daily, closed Sunday in low season) offers that oh-so-commmon combination of coffee, pasta, and laundry. The latter costs US$1.20 per kilo (2.2 pounds) for next day pickup, or $2 per kilo for same-day service, both with a three-kilo (6.6-pound) minimum.

GETTING THERE AND AROUND

By public transportation take a *combi* from Cancún, Playa del Carmen, or Tulum (US$2). Let the driver know where you're going and he'll drop you off on the side of the highway. From there, it's 500 meters (0.3 mile) into town. Arriving by car you'll pass through a large control gate, but no one who looks like a tourist is stopped.

In Puerto Aventuras, you can walk just about everywhere, as virtually all shops and services are centered around the marina.

Xpu-Há

This long, picturesque beach has clusters of development on either end and practically nothing in between. It seems only a matter of time before the owners of this enviable stretch of sand give their blessing to a megaresort, but for now it's a gorgeous and peaceful spot where you could easily while away the whole day, or several.

SPORTS AND RECREATION

Beach Clubs

La Playa Xpu-Há (entrance at Carr. Cancún–Tulum Km. 265, tel. 984/106-0024) is a bustling club that offers a slew of classic beach activities, including parasailing, fishing, banana boats, snorkeling, and kayaking, all at standard prices. On weekends, there's a US$2.50 per person "toll" at the entrance, charged by the landowner for upkeep of the access road. You get it back, though, as a credit on restaurant bills over US$10.

Just down the beach, **Xpu-Há Bonanza** (entrance at Carr. Cancún–Tulum Km. 265, tel. 984/116-4733) has a much quieter scene, with a small number of beach chairs and umbrellas, yet close enough to La Playa to take advantage of the restaurant and water activities there. Parking and clean bathroom facilities are available.

Snorkeling

In addition to the ocean reef, there's great snorkeling in the numerous cenotes along the inland side of Hwy. 307, including a cluster just north of Xpu-Há. They vary in size, but most are like large ponds, some with high or overhanging limestone walls, and all filled with cool crystalline water—heaven on a hot day. The cenote floor is often a jumble of stone slabs and in places quite deep—some even have gaping underwater caves that descend out of sight.

© LIZA PRADO

With a view like this, it's no wonder travelers come back to Xpu-Há so often.

The cenotes near Xpu-Há are not, however, the huge stalactite-laden caverns you may have seen in photos; for those, head south to Hidden Worlds or Dos Ojos cenote parks, both near Tulum.

Cristalino Cenote (Hwy. 307, 2 km/1.2 mi north of Xpu-Há, 8 A.M.–6 P.M. daily) charges US$4 adult, US$2 child, with no rental gear available. Much of this half moon–shaped cenote is shallow and covered in algae, but one section extends under a deep overhanging rock ceiling.

Jardín de Edén (formerly Ponderosa Cenote, Hwy. 307, 1.75 km/1 mi north of Xpu-Há, 8 A.M.–5 P.M. Sun.–Fri.) is much larger than most cenotes—almost like a small lake—with a craggy floor that makes for fun snorkeling. At one end, the floor falls away into a deep underwater cave, where you can see divers emerging—or disappearing—into the abyss, their halogen lights piercing the shadows. A six-meter cliff is fun to jump off, just be alert for divers who may be coming up. Between cave-diving classes, snorkeling groups, and independent travelers, Jardín del Edén can get busy but is generally big enough

to make a stop here worthwhile. Admission is US$4 adult, US$2 child, US$3 to rent mask and snorkel, and US$3 for a life vest.

At **Cenote Azul** (8 A.M.–6 P.M. daily, US$5 adult, US$3 child, US$3 mask and snorkel, US$3 life vest) a few large pools and a section of overhanging rock are the highlights, and walkways along the edges facilitate getting in and out.

Scuba Diving

Bahía Divers (tel. 984/120-1546, www.bahiadivers.com) operates out of a small hut a short distance down the beach from La Playa. It offers the full gamut of fun dives (including ocean, cenote, night, and Cozumel trips), plus certification courses and snorkeling and fishing trips, all with the advantage of small groups and personal service. (They also provide transport to and from your hotel, which is very handy.) Ocean dives cost US$39/70 for one/two tanks, and cenote dives are US$110 for two tanks; diving gear rental is US$15–20 per day. Snorkeling trips cost US$35–75 per person, depending where you go—reef, cenote, lagoon, or a combination of the three.

ACCOMMODATIONS AND FOOD

Xpu-Há Bonanza (entrance at Carr. Cancún–Tulum Km. 265, tel. 984/116-4733, US$5 pp camping, US$15 RVs, US$60 s/d) is a low-key beachfront spot with room for camping and RVs, plus eight large hotel rooms. The latter have two beds and two hammocks and clean cold-water bathrooms, but lack for natural light. Travelers with tents can set up in the sand under a palm tree, and have access to clean-ish shared bathrooms. To get here, look for a narrow dirt road with a small sign, just south of the Catalonia Royal Tulum resort.

Sitting on 50 lush acres at the northern end of Playa Xpu-Há, **Hotel Esencia** (Carr. Cancún–Tulum Km. 265, tel. 984/873-4830, toll-free Mex. tel. 800/561-9162, www.hotelesencia.com, US$440–1,430 s/d with fan) is a luxurious private estate turned resort. It boasts 29 gorgeous stark white rooms, each with a plunge pool and modern amenities like flat-screen TVs and surround sound audio systems (bring your iPod). The beach is just steps away, and has plenty of *palapa* shades and loungers so there's no need to claim a spot before the sun rises. The hotel's gourmet restaurant faces the Caribbean; guests can enjoy a daily continental breakfast as well as afternoon tea here. There's also a full-service spa on-site and yoga instruction is offered every morning. Service, as expected, is impeccable.

INFORMATION AND SERVICES

There are no services in Xpu-Há, save what's available to guests at Hotel Esencia and Catolonia Royal Tulum resort. For Internet, laundry, ATM, and other services, head to Akumal or Puerto Aventuras.

GETTING THERE AND AROUND

Each of the listings for Xpu-Há has its own access road, marked with large or small signs, and located at or near Km. 265 on the main coastal highway. Catolonia Royal Tulum resort is the largest and most obvious landmark; the other access roads are within a few hundred yards. La Plaza and Xpu-Há Bonanza, at the southern end of the beach, are the best access points if you're only staying the day.

Akumal

Unreachable by land until the 1960s, Akumal (literally, Place of the Turtle) is a quiet, upscale community that has developed on two bays: Akumal and Half Moon. It's a low-key place with sand roads and dozens of condominiums and rental homes. The beach in town is decent—if you don't mind the boats parked on the sand—and the one around Half Moon Bay is calm though rocky in places. Just off-shore, a spectacular portion of barrier reef makes for great diving and snorkeling and protects Akumal's bays from the open sea.

A short distance south of Akumal proper is Aventuras Akumal, another small bayside

Akumal's lovely and busy main beach

© GARY CHANDLER

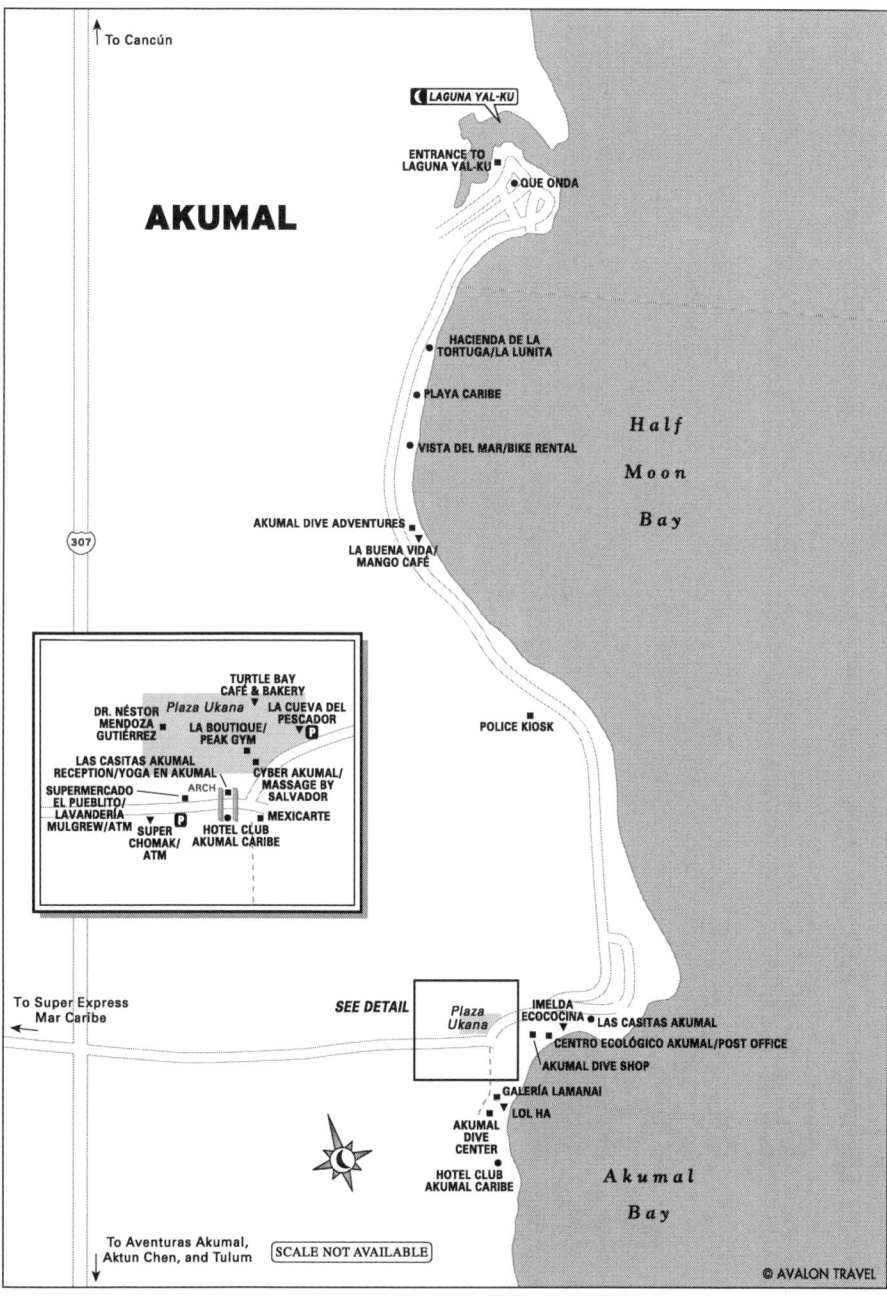

To Cancún

LAGUNA YAL-KU

ENTRANCE TO
LAGUNA YAL-KU

QUE ONDA

AKUMAL

HACIENDA DE LA
TORTUGA/LA LUNITA

PLAYA CARIBE

Half

VISTA DEL MAR/BIKE RENTAL

Moon

AKUMAL DIVE ADVENTURES

Bay

LA BUENA VIDA/
MANGO CAFÉ

307

TURTLE BAY
CAFÉ & BAKERY

DR. NÉSTOR   *Plaza Ukana*   LA CUEVA DEL
MENDOZA   PESCADOR
GUTIÉRREZ   LA BOUTIQUE/
              PEAK GYM

POLICE KIOSK

LAS CASITAS AKUMAL
RECEPTION/YOGA EN AKUMAL

ARCH   CYBER AKUMAL/
SUPERMERCADO   MASSAGE BY
EL PUEBLITO/   SALVADOR
LAVANDERÍA
MULGREW/ATM   SUPER   MEXICARTE
              CHOMAK/
              ATM   HOTEL CLUB
              AKUMAL CARIBE

To Super Express
Mar Caribe

SEE DETAIL   *Plaza*   IMELDA
                  Ukana ECOCOCINA   LAS CASITAS AKUMAL

CENTRO ECOLÓGICO AKUMAL/POST OFFICE

AKUMAL DIVE SHOP

GALERÍA LAMANAI

LOL HA

AKUMAL
DIVE
CENTER

HOTEL CLUB
AKUMAL CARIBE

Akumal

Bay

To Aventuras Akumal,
Aktun Chen, and Tulum   SCALE NOT AVAILABLE

© AVALON TRAVEL

THE RIVIERA MAYA

development. It doesn't have the town-like feel or activity that Akumal does, but two good condo-hotels and a truly gorgeous beach make this a tempting alternative. Aventuras Akumal has a separate access road from the highway, and walking there along the beach takes about 45 minutes.

SIGHTS
Beaches
Akumal Bay—the one right in front of town—has a long, slow-curving shoreline, with soft sand shaded by palm trees. The water is beautiful but a bit rocky underfoot, and you should be aware of boat traffic when swimming or snorkeling. Half Moon Bay can also be nice for swimming and snorkeling, but the shoreline is rocky in many parts; where there is beach, it is mostly narrow and covered with sea plants that have washed ashore.

(Laguna Yal-Ku
At the mouth of an elbow-shaped lagoon at the north end of Akumal, an endless upwelling of underground river water collides with the tireless flow of seawater—the result is a great place to snorkel, teeming with fish and plants adapted to this unique hybrid environment. Once a secret snorkeler's getaway, Laguna Yal-Ku (8 A.M.–5:30 P.M. daily, US$9 adult, US$6 child, US$15 snorkel gear, US$2 locker) now has a parking lot and a spot in every guidebook and tour group itinerary—come before 10 A.M. or anytime on Sunday for the least traffic. You can snorkel in the lagoon's broad mouth, or up the narrow channel to its source. If possible, use a T-shirt or wetsuit instead of sunscreen—even the biodegradable kind can collect on plants and coral. The lagoon's edges are dotted with various intriguing bronze sculptures by Mexican artist Alejandro Echeverría.

Centro Ecológico Akumal
Next to Akumal Dive Shop, the Akumal Ecological Center (CEA, tel. 984/875-9095, www.ceakumal.org, 9 A.M.–6 P.M. Mon.–Fri., 9 A.M.–1 P.M. Sat.) is a nonprofit founded in

A bronze statue contemplates a pair of snorkelers in Laguna Yal-Ku in Akumal.

SEA TURTLES

All eight of the world's sea-turtle species are considered endangered, thanks to a combination of antiquated fishing practices, habitat destruction – particularly of the beaches where they nest – and a taste for turtle meat, eggs, and shells that has proved hard to break in many coastal communities. Four turtle species – hawksbill, Kemp's ridley, green, and loggerhead – nest on the shores of the Yucatán Peninsula, and until relatively recently they were a common supplement to the regional diet. Turtles make easy prey, especially females clambering on shore to lay eggs. They are killed for their meat, fat, eggs (which are eaten or saved for medicinal purposes),

and shells, used to make amber-like jewelry, combs, and other crafts.

Various environmental protection organizations in the Yucatán have joined forces with the Mexican government to protect sea turtles and their habitat; they have developed breeding programs and maintain strict surveillance of known nesting beaches to stop poaching. It is strictly prohibited to capture and trade sea turtles or their products in Mexico. Travelers can do their part to protect these ancient creatures by not buying products like leather, oils, or tortoise-shell products, or foods made with their eggs or meat.

1993 to monitor the health of Akumal's ecosystems, particularly related to coral and sea turtles. During turtle nesting season (May–July) you can join CEA volunteers on nighttime turtle walks, covering about two kilometers (1.25 miles) of beach, looking for new nests and helping move eggs to protected hatcheries. From August to October, visitors can help release a batch of hatchlings into the sea (9 P.M. Mon.–Fri.). Stop by the center for more details and to sign up; turtle outings and activities are free but a US$10 donation is appreciated. The center also has free displays and frequent evening lectures on ocean ecology (in high season).

CEA also operates long-term volunteer projects on reef monitoring, sea-turtles monitoring, and environmental education projects. Volunteers stay in the center's comfortable dorms, with kitchen and Internet access; minimum age is 21 and some fees are required. See the website for details.

Aktun Chen

Maya for 'Cave with an Underground River,' Aktun Chen (Carr. Cancún–Tulum Km. 107, tel. 984/806-4962 or 984/109-2094 in Playa del Carmen, www.aktunchen.com, 9 A.M.–5 P.M. daily, until 6 P.M. in summer, last tour 30 mins before closing, US$26 adult,

US$14 child under 10) is indeed that, and more. The price is awfully steep, but the experience is certainly memorable. The cave system has a breathtaking array of stalactites and stalagmites, and a 12-meter-deep (40-foot) cenote filled with crystalline water at the end; lighting and a pathway make it accessible to all.

Leaving the cave, you can check out the park's numerous animal enclosures, with spider monkeys, toucans, and more; a zip line and a cenote for swimming are in the works as well. Tours are offered in English and Spanish and last about 90 minutes. Most hotels offer trips here that include transportation, or you can go independently—look for the turnoff just across from Aventuras Akumal, and continue three kilometers (1.9 miles) to the entrance. Mosquito repellent and a bottle of water are recommended. You'll encounter the least crowds before 11 A.M. and on weekends.

SHOPPING

Mexicarte (9 A.M.–9 P.M. daily) is the small bright-pink shop just inside the arches on your right. The owner hand-selects the best folk art from around the region and country. Prices are high, but so is the quality and artisanship.

Galería Lamanai (tel. 984/875-9055, www.galerialamani.com, 8 A.M.–9 P.M. daily)

offers similar wares, both in quality and price. The shop is located on the beach near Snack Bar Lol Ha.

SPORTS AND RECREATION
Scuba Diving

Some of the area's first scuba divers waded into the waves right here at Akumal Bay, and the area has been special to the sport ever since. While not as spectacular as other areas along the Riviera Maya, Akumal's diving is easy and fun, with a mellow current and few profiles that go below 20 meters (66 feet). The reef is predominantly boulder coral, which isn't as picturesque as other types, but still it teems with tropical fish and plant life. Visibility is decent by Caribbean standards—great by everyone else's—averaging 10–30 meters (33–99 feet).

Founded more than 30 years ago, **Akumal Dive Shop** (tel. 984/875-9032, www.akumal.com, 8 A.M.–5 P.M. daily) was the first dive shop in the Riviera Maya, long before anyone called it that. Still right on the beach, the shop offers fun dives and various certification courses in both open water and cave/cavern diving. Divers can take one- or two-tank reef dives (US$50/70), cavern or cenote dives (US$75/140), or buy packages of 4 or 10 dives for US$140/290. Fun dives do not include equipment rental (US$18/day, US$70/week). Open-water certification courses take 3–4 days and cost US$485, equipment and materials included.

Down the beach a short distance, **Akumal Dive Center** (tel. 984/875-9025, www.akumaldivecenter.com, 8 A.M.–5 P.M. daily) has operated in Akumal almost as long and offers the same dives and courses at comparable prices.

On Half Moon Bay, **Akumal Dive Adventures** (next to La Buena Vida restaurant, tel. 984/875-9157, toll-free U.S. tel. 877/425-8625, www.akumaldiveadventures.com, 8 A.M.–5 P.M. daily) offers somewhat lower prices than the other shops, as well as dive and accommodation packages starting at three nights lodging and four reef dives for US$290/390 per person double/single

occupancy. Rooms are at the affiliated Vista del Mar hotel.

Aventuras Akumal has excellent diving and snorkeling as well, with a calm bay and less traffic than Akumal proper. **Aquatech Dive Center** (Villas DeRosa, tel. 984/875-9020, toll-free U.S. tel. 866/619-9050, www.cenotes.com) has many years of experience and offers a complete range of dives and courses, with special emphasis on cenote and cave diving. Reef dives run US$40/60 for one/two tanks, while cenote dives are US$65/120. Open-water certification is US$350 per person—check the website for details on cavern and cave diving instruction. Equipment is included in courses, but not fun dives (US$35–40 per day for the full kit). Multi-dive packages, night dives, and fishing excursions are also available.

Snorkeling

Laguna Yal-Ku (8 A.M.–5:30 P.M. daily, US$9 adult, US$6 child, US$14 snorkel gear, US$2 locker) is a favorite among many snorkelers for its large area, calm water, and unique mix of fresh- and saltwater ecosystems. Look for several modern sculptures standing somewhat incongruously along the lagoon's edges.

The northern end of **Akumal Bay** also has fine snorkeling, reachable right from the beach. It's a great little nook of fairly shallow water, where tropical fish dart about a labyrinth of rocks, boulder coral, and plant life. Fishing boats do not pass through here, another reason it's good for snorkeling, but be alert to currents pulling you out of the safe area and into boat channels. Likewise, some snorkelers make their way toward the large buoy at the edge of the bay, not realizing it marks a channel that boats use to get through the reef. Be smart and steer clear. Half Moon Bay has some good shore snorkeling as well.

You can rent **snorkel gear** at any of Akumal's dive shops for around US$12 a day or US$60 a week. Rentals at Yal-Ku cost US$14 and can only be used on-site. The dive shops also offer **guided snorkel tours**, which run 1–3 hours, depending on the number of sites you visit, and cost US$10–40 per person, including gear.

Sailing

Akumal Dive Shop (tel. 984/875-9032, www.akumal.com, 8 A.M.–5 P.M. daily) offers a popular Robinson Crusoe cruise: a five-hour excursion on a catamaran sailboat, with stops for fishing and snorkeling (US$85 including lunch and equipment). Or try the two-hour Sunset Cruise, which doesn't include fishing and snorkeling, but offers beautiful evening views of the bay.

Sport Fishing

Dive shops also offer fishing tours, varying somewhat in length and group size according to the type of boat that's available. Expect to pay between US$90 and US$150 for a two-to-three-hour tour for 2–4 anglers. Trips typically include equipment, tackle, and beverages, and longer outings can be arranged. Fishing is excellent year-round, but the best months for trolling are April–June when sailfish and marlin are most numerous and active.

To schedule a tour, contact Akumal Dive Shop (tel. 984/875-9032, www.akumal.com, 8 A.M.–5 P.M. daily), **Akumal Dive Center** (tel. 984/875-9025, www.akumaldivecenter.com, 8 A.M.–5 P.M. daily), or **Akumal Dive Adventures** (tel. 984/875-9157, toll-free U.S. tel. 877/425-8625, www.akumaldiveadventures.com, 8 A.M.–5 P.M. daily).

Spas and Gyms

In a breezy upstairs studio in the archway to town, **Yoga en Akumal** (tel. 984/875-9114 or 998/849-4691, leticiaak@prodigy.net.mex) offers hatha classes for all experience levels. Sessions are 90 minutes long (7–8:30 P.M. and 8:30–10 P.M. Tues.–Wed. and Fri.) and cost US$15 per class, US$75 for a two-week pass, or US$125 for a month.

Peak Gym (Plaza Ukana, 1st Fl., tel. 984/875-9208, 8 A.M.–7 P.M. Mon.–Sat.) has a small air-conditioned exercise space that's crammed with free weights and machines. Stationary bikes are the only cardio option—there are no stairsteppers or ellipticals, unfortunately. Day passes cost US$10, 3-day passes

US$27, weekly rates US$46, and monthly membership is US$60.

For a breezy outdoor massage, try **Massage by Salvador** (Plaza Ukana, 2nd Fl., no phone, Mon.–Sat., US$60/hour). Salvador speaks English and has two weeks' worth of sign-up sheets outside his door; just stop by and sign up for an appointment.

ACCOMMODATIONS

Akumal draws a number of long-term visitors and has a large number of fully equipped condos and villas, in addition to ordinary hotels. There's no hostel, but backpackers might be able snag a dorm room at CEA.

In Town

Centro Ecológico Akumal (CEA, tel. 984/875-9095, www.ceakumal.org, 9 A.M.–6 P.M. Mon.–Fri., 9 A.M.–1 P.M. Sat.) has several large comfortable dorms—most even have air-conditioning—and a well-outfitted communal kitchen. CEA's volunteers have priority for the rooms, and they are usually full, but if not they're available to walk-ins for US$15 a night. It's a long shot, but definitely worth asking.

Hotel Club Akumal Caribe (reception in the arches at the entrance to town, tel. 915/584-3552, toll-free U.S. tel. 800/351-1622, toll-free Canada tel. 800/343-1440, www.hotelakumalcaribe.com, US$123 s/d bungalow with a/c, US$156 s/d room with a/c) was the first hotel in Akumal, when it was used by members of a local diving and conservation club. The bungalows are roomy and affordable—and therefore popular with families—but are in need of a serious remodel. Rooms in the hotel section are much more appealing, with whitewashed walls, air-conditioning, refrigerator, and private balcony. Most have ocean views; some have kitchenettes. The main complaint here is the beds, which range from firm to rock hard. The hotel has a well-kempt swimming pool and palm-shaded beach area, including a guest-only section. A good restaurant, a pizzeria, and a full-service dive shop are also on-site.

On the eastern end of the beach in town, **Las Casitas Akumal** (tel. 984/875-9071, toll-free U.S./Canada tel. 800/525-8625, www.lascasitasakumal.com) has 18 airy furnished condominiums with two bedrooms, two baths, living room, fully equipped kitchen, and private patio. Some have two floors and space for six people; all have ocean views and direct access to a semiprivate section of the beach. High-season rates range US$330–375 per night; holidays rates are higher, while rates drop significantly in May, September, and October. Reservations must be made for a minimum of seven nights and begin on a Saturday.

Half Moon Bay

One nice thing about staying in Half Moon Bay—in addition to the beautiful ocean views and great snorkeling—is that you're within walking distance of the center as well as Laguna Yal-Ku.

Located midway around the bay, **Vista del Mar** (tel. 984/875-9060, toll-free U.S. tel. 888/425-8625, www.akumalinfo.com, US$100/125 d/q hotel room, US$205–325 condos for 2–7 people) has spacious one-, two-, and three-bedroom condominiums, plus standard hotel rooms, all overlooking a lovely stretch of beach. The 15 condos have long balconies or porches, huge fully equipped kitchens, separate living and dining rooms, and master bedrooms with king-size beds. Modern amenities include flat-screen TVs, mini-air-conditioners, in-room safes, wireless Internet, and some whirlpool tubs. (Oh, and daily maid service too!) Mexican decor like Talavera tiles, bright hand-woven bedspreads, and tapestries lend the place even more charm. The 16 oceanfront hotel rooms are smaller, but still comfortable and a bit less expensive. All accommodations share a well-tended beach with lounge chairs and *palapa* shades.

Hacienda de la Tortuga (tel. 984/875-9068, www.haciendatortuga.com) has just 16 rooms and cultivates a quiet relaxed atmosphere. Roomy one-bedroom (US$150) and two-bedroom (US$200) condos all have huge windows overlooking the Caribbean, plus a living

room, fully equipped kitchen, king-size bed(s), and air-conditioning in the bedrooms. Each is uniquely decorated, many with fine Mexican artwork and homey touches like a well-stocked bookcase. There's a nice pool just steps from the beach, and a classy Mexican restaurant, **La Lunita,** that gets good reviews.

At the north end of Akumal and just a block from Laguna Yal-Ku, **Que Onda** (Caleta Yal-Ku, tel. 984/875-9101, www.queondaakumal.com, US$80 s/d, US$145–170 suite) has seven rooms, each lovingly decorated with tile floors, beautiful fabrics, and unique works of art, and two suites, including a split-level unit with wood floors and terrific views of the Caribbean and Yal-Ku. All face a verdant garden and a pool in the middle of the property. None have air-conditioning; the 1st-floor units can get a bit stuffy while upstairs rooms have terraces and sea breezes. Use of bicycles and snorkel gear are included in the rates—a big plus—and guests get 50 percent off admission to Laguna Yal-Ku. The Italian restaurant here can get busy.

Aventuras Akumal

Villas DeRosa (tel. 984/875-9020, toll-free U.S. tel. 866/619-9050, www.cenotes.com, US$80 s/d, US$150 one-bedroom, US$205–230 two-bedroom, US$260 three-bedroom) offers hotel rooms with garden views and spacious condominiums with ocean views and private balconies. All units have air-conditioning, cable TV, wireless Internet, and stereos, and condos have fully equipped kitchens as well. The bedrooms can feel a bit dark, but you're literally steps from a beautiful beach and the blue Caribbean water. The resort boasts a full-service dive shop, with a special emphasis on cenote diving; dive/accommodation packages are available.

Smaller and cozier than the DeRosa, **Villa Las Brisas** (tel. 984/875-9263, www.aventuras-akumal.com, US$90 s/d, US$100 studio, US$150 one-bedroom condo, US$215 two-bedroom condo) has just three units (two of which can be combined to make the two-bedroom condo)—all spacious, spotless, and meticulously furnished, down to a stocked spice rack in the kitchen. Opened in 1998, the condos have large terraces with hammocks and stunning views; the smaller units have balconies that overlook a tidy garden. With comfortable beds, modern Mexican-style furnishings, and room to stretch out in, it's easy to feel at home here. Families are very welcome. Beach chairs and umbrellas are free, snorkel gear can be rented (US$5 per day), and there's a simple minimart at the entrance (8 A.M.–4 P.M. Mon–Sat.).

Rental Properties

The majority of rooms for rent in Akumal are in privately owned homes and condos, especially along Half Moon Bay. Most are managed and rented by one of various property management companies; browse the listings of several agencies to get the best selection. Some reliable agencies include **Caribbean Fantasy** (www.caribbfan.com, toll-free U.S. tel. 800/523-6618), **Akumal Villas** (www.akumalvillas.com, U.S. tel. 678/528-1775), **Akumal Rentals** (www.akumal-rentals.com, tel. 998/185-6222), and **Loco Gringo** (www.locogringo.com, no phone).

FOOD
In Town

Lol Ha (Hotel Akumal Caribe, tel. 984/875-9013, www.hotelakumalcaribe.com, 7:30–11 A.M. and 6:30–10 P.M. daily, closed Oct.–mid-Nov., US$12–35) is Akumal's finest restaurant, with a beautiful wood and stucco dining room topped with a high *palapa* roof that opens onto a pleasant veranda. Expect excellent seafood and Mexican and American specialties, including prime USDA steaks, grilled ahi tuna, and flambé specials prepared tableside. The restaurant hosts Mexican folk dance performances on Mondays, flamenco on Wednesday, and jazz on Friday—a small per-person cover charge is added to the bill. Reservations are highly recommended.

Next door, **Snack Bar Lol Ha** (11:30 A.M.–8 P.M. daily, US$8–14) serves the best hamburgers on the beach, and tasty tacos too (the *tacos de cochinita* are particularly good). Three 32-inch

TVs always have a sporting event on, whether Monday Night Football, March Madness, or the Kentucky Derby; hundreds of people turn out for the annual Super Bowl and Academy Awards parties (proceeds of which go to local community groups). Kids will love the adjacent game room with air hockey and foosball.

For a fresh, healthy meal, try **Imelda Ecococina** (no phone, 8 A.M.–3 P.M. daily, US$3–6) next to Centro Ecológico Akumal. Breakfast options include eggs, omelets, pancakes, French toast, and more. For lunch, the *comida corrida* comes with a choice of main plate and a side dish or two. On Mondays and Thursdays the restaurant hosts a popular Maya buffet (US$20, 7 P.M.) followed by *cumbia* tunes and dancing.

In Plaza Ukana, **(Turtle Bay Café & Bakery** (tel. 984/875-9138, 7 A.M.–3 P.M. and 6–9 P.M. Tues.–Sat., 7 A.M.–3 P.M. Sun.–Mon., US$5–18) offers scrumptious creations such as grilled portobello mushroom burgers, achiote chicken, and summer burritos. For breakfast, think French toast, eggs Benedict, or a fruit plate with yogurt and granola. Enjoy your meal surrounded by palm trees, either in the outdoor *palapa*-roofed dining room or on the porch of the main building.

For fresh seafood, check out **La Cueva del Pescador** (Plaza Ukana, tel. 984/875-9205, noon–10 P.M.daily, US$5–25). Sink your teeth into fish kabobs, shrimp prepared nine different ways (e.g., grilled, à la tequila, with curry salsa, and so on), and lobster—all caught the day you order it. The bar is an especially popular spot on weekends.

For groceries, the best prices are across from the Akumal turnoff on Hwy. 307 in **Super Express Mar Caribe** (7 A.M.–11 P.M. daily); look for the store about 100 meters (328 feet) west of the highway. Otherwise, just outside the arch **Super Chomak** and **Supermercado El Pueblito** (both 7 A.M.–9 P.M. daily) charge an arm and a leg for canned and dried food, soups and pastas, fresh and packaged meat, booze, and basics like sunscreen and film. All have ATM machines inside, and El Pueblito accepts credit cards. They also sell fresh fruit

THE RIVIERA MAYA

and veggies, but you may find a better selection at the **farmers market** held Wednesdays and Saturdays in Plaza Ukana.

Half Moon Bay

A fantastic flying serpent skeleton greets diners at **La Buena Vida** (Vista del Mar, tel. 984/875-9061, www.akumalinfo.com/restaurant.htm, 11 A.M.–11 P.M.daily, US$6–27), where clients enjoy the varied menu—from hamburgers to shrimp ceviche—under *palapa*-shaded tables on the beach. If you've already had lunch, consider just stopping in for a drink at the swing-lined bar; happy hour typically runs 5–7 P.M.

Next door, the brightly painted **Mango Café** (no phone, 7 A.M.–noon daily) serves up a good variety of breakfasts on the beach—think breakfast burritos, bagels, lattes, and fresh fruit smoothies. Look for it just before the Vista del Mar condominiums.

La Lunita (Hacienda de la Tortuga, tel. 984/875-9070, www.lalunita-akumal.com, 5–10:30 P.M. Mon.–Sat., US$8–24) is an intimate bistro serving gourmet Mexican and Maya specialties. Seafood is king here, though there are plenty of options for vegetarians and serious meat eaters. With only a handful of tables, some overlooking the Caribbean, La Lunita is a perfect place for a romantic dinner—just be sure to make reservations.

If you're in the mood for Italian, try the open-air restaurant at the hotel **Que Onda** (7–11 A.M., noon–4 P.M., and 5:30–10 P.M. Wed.–Mon., US$7–18). The homemade linguine comes with a wide choice of sauces, from gorgonzola to curry shrimp. The lasagna is famously tasty, though a bit pricey. For dessert, try the chocolate mousse.

INFORMATION AND SERVICES

Tourist Information

Akumal doesn't have an official tourist office, but it's a small town and you can probably find what you're looking for by asking the first person you see. If that fails, the folks at Centro Ecológico Akumal (CEA, tel. 984/875-9095,

www.ceakumal.org, 9 A.M.–6 P.M. Mon.–Fri., 9 A.M.–1 P.M. Sat.) are friendly and well informed, and most speak English.

Emergency Services

For an English-speaking physician, call or stop by the offices of general practitioner **Dr. Néstor Mendoza Gutiérrez** (Plaza Ukana, tel. 984/875-4051, 8 A.M.–4 P.M. Mon.–Sat., after-hours emergencies cell tel. 044-984/806-4616). For major medical matters, head to Playa del Carmen. The **police** can be reached by calling 060 from any public phone.

Money

There are cash machines inside both of Akumal's small supermarkets, just outside the arch: Super Chomak and Supermercado El Pueblito (both 7 A.M.–9 P.M. daily).

Media and Communications

The **post office** (9:30 A.M.–3 P.M. Tues. and Thurs.) is inside the Centro Ecológico Akumal, in the center of town. **Cyber Akumal** (Plaza Ukana, tel. 984/875-9313, 7 A.M.–1 A.M., until 9 P.M. only in low season) is Akumal's go-to Internet café, located just past the arches as you enter town. Internet is fast, but runs a hefty US$0.10 a minute, while international calls are around US$0.50 per minute. In high season, there are discounts on Internet use and calls after 9 P.M.

Laundry

Next to Supermercado El Pueblito, **Lavandería Mulgrew** (7 A.M.–1 P.M. and 5–7 P.M. Mon.–Sat.) charges US$2.50 a kilogram (2.2 pounds) and will provide same-day service if you drop off your load before 8:30 A.M. (two-kilogram/4.4-pound minimum).

GETTING THERE AND AROUND

The turnoff to Akumal is between Kms. 254 and 255 on the main highway. For Aventuras Akumal, the access road is just south of the main Akumal entrance; look for the sign to Hotel Villas DeRosa, as the community itself isn't well signed.

© GARY CHANDLER

THE RIVIERA MAYA

A small inland cenote is another reason to love the wonderfully undeveloped Playa Xcacel.

Bus and *Combi*

Combis and second-class buses stop at the Akumal turnoff, but it's a kilometer (0.6 mile) walk into town. Likewise, you can manage the center area by foot, but walking to and from Half Moon Bay can be long, hot, and dusty. Biking is a good alternative.

Combis and second-class buses also stop at the Aventuras Akumal entrance; it's only about 500 meters (0.3 mile) into the community from there.

Taxi

Taxis gather near the Super Chomak grocery store at the entrance of Akumal, just outside of the arches. A ride from town to Laguna Yal-Ku costs US$3.

Bicycle

The condo-hotel **Vista del Mar** (Half Moon Bay, tel. 984/875-9060) rents decent bikes for US$6 per day.

◖ PLAYA XCACEL

For all the breakneck construction along the Riviera Maya, much of the coastline remains virtually untouched, including some gorgeous stretches of white-sand beach. Playa Xcacel (Hwy. 307 Km. 247.5, 8 A.M.–6 P.M. daily, US$2) is one of those, a gently curving band of thick white sand, with only a small parking lot, restrooms, and changing area, and popular with local residents. Xcacel's pristine state is thanks in part to the fact that sea turtles nest here, and development is restricted by federal law. Along the inland edge of the beach are scores of wood blades with dates on them, marking where and when sea turtles laid eggs; needless to say, do not move the markers or disturb the nests! A small freshwater cenote is located down a slippery path, about 350 meters (1,148 feet) south of the main entrance. The turnoff to Playa Xcacel is easy to miss, but located 11 kilometers (7 miles) north of Tulum between the Xel-Há ecopark and Chemuyil community.

Tankah Tres

Tucked innocuously between Akumal and Tulum, Tankah Tres sees only a fraction of the tourist traffic that its better-known neighbors do. But that's just the way visitors to this little stretch of coastline prefer it, enjoying excellent snorkeling, diving, and pretty (if not spectacular) beaches, with a sense of isolation that's hard to find in these parts. The area has three small bays, and the scattered hotels, villas, and private homes along their shores were once connected (together and to the highway) by a U-shaped access road. But new development cut the *U* right in half; the southern entrance is still marked Tankah Tres, while the northern entrance has a sign for Oscar y Lalo restaurant and Bahías de Punta Soliman. You have to return to the highway to get from one side to the other.

SIGHTS
Playa Tankah
The handful of hotels here all have pretty beachfronts along Tankah's three sandy bays.

If you aren't staying at one of the hotels, Casa Cenote (1.5 km/0.9 mi from the turnoff, tel. 998/874-5170, www.casacenote.com) allows non-guests to enjoy the hotel beach and lounge chairs if they order something at the restaurant.

Cenote Manatí
Across from Casa Cenote hotel (1.5 km/0.9 mi from the turnoff, tel. 998/874-5170, www.casacenote.com, sunrise–sunset)—and frequently referred to by the same name—Cenote Manatí (free) is actually a series of interconnected cenotes and lagoons, extending from the road well inland. (An underground channel drains into the ocean.) The crystal-clear water, winding channels, and tangle of rocks, trees, and freshwater plants along the edges and bottom all make for terrific snorkeling. Look for schools of tiny fish near the surface, and some bigger ones farther down.

The restaurant **Oscar y Lalo** (tel. 984/115-9965 or 984/804-4189) rents snorkel

Tankah Tres is a quiet getaway with a refreshingly unmanicured beach.

© LIZA PRADO

THE RIVIERA MAYA

gear (US$6/day) and kayaks (US$9/hour); it also offers snorkel and kayaking tours into the lagoon that extends behind the property.

ACCOMMODATIONS

The northern entrance to Tankah Tres extends almost to the beach before forking; to the left is **Oscar y Lalo** (tel. 984/115-9965 or 984/804-4189), a restaurant and campsite on an isolated palm tree–lined beach. Here, you can set up a tent among the coconut trees for US$5 per person and feel, if only for a night or two, as if you are on an idyllic deserted island (that happens to have a bathroom with running water, of course). When the restaurant closes at 8 P.M. the place is yours, starry night and all. Be sure to bring mosquito nets in the rainy season.

Five spacious rooms with murals of Maya temples make up the **Tankah Inn** (southern entrance, 1.1 km/0.6 mi from the turnoff, U.S. tel. 918/582-3743, www.tankah.com, US$145 s/d with a/c). Right on the beach, each room has tile floors, a private terrace, and ocean views; all come equipped with five-gallon jugs of water and remote-controlled air-conditioning. A breezy common room has sweeping views of the Caribbean—comfy chairs and tables, a stereo, lots of board games, and an honor bar make this a popular place to hang out, though the beach, with its lounge chairs and hammocks, is a tempting alternative. A full breakfast is included, as is wireless Internet and the use of sea kayaks.

Casa Cenote (southern entrance, 1.5 km/0.9 mi from the turnoff, tel. 998/874-5170, www.casacenote.com, US$196 s/d with a/c) was for many years the only life on this stretch of beach; more hotels have popped up, but this remains a favorite of old-timers and newcomers alike. All seven rooms have air-conditioning, one or two large beds, wireless Internet, and a sliding glass door that opens onto a small patio with fine ocean views. Decor is fairly low-key, save the large stucco relief of a Maya god in each room. The hotel built a new pool after Hurricane Wilma, and Cenote Manatí is just across the street. The hotel does its part for the

earth by collecting rainwater and using natural wastewater processing. Breakfast is included.

Blue Sky Hotel (southern entrance, 1.7 km/1 mi from the turnoff, tel. 984/801-4004, toll-free U.S./Canada tel. 877/792-9237, www.blueskymexico.com, US$165–255 with a/c) offers six breezy units with views of the Caribbean. All are modern and decorated with Mexican flair—mostly high-end folk art with lots of recessed lighting. A nice pool opens onto the beach, where there are plenty of toys—kayaks, boogie boards, and snorkel gear—for guests to use. The hotel's *palapa* restaurant is one of the best around.

Slice of Paradise (southern entrance, 2 km/1.5 mi from the turnoff, www.sliceofparadise.com, US$100–145 s/d, US$2,000/week house with a/c) lives up to its name with two *palapa*-roofed *cabañas:* a cozy casita with full-size kitchen, and a spacious beach house (sleeps two) with sunken living room, a kitchen, and dramatic bay windows. Both have air-conditioning, simple but tasteful decor, and are just steps from a nice stretch of beach.

FOOD

Near the northern entrance to town, **Oscar y Lalo** (tel. 984/804-4819 or 984/115-9965, www.restauranteoscarylalo.com, 10 A.M.–8 P.M. daily, US$7–32) is an ocean-side restaurant that serves excellent fresh seafood. All dishes come with fried banana, french fries, beans, and rice. Main dishes are definitely pricey—four-to-six-person specials run US$20–30 per person—but the view and the monster portions more than make up for it.

The restaurant at **Casa Cenote** (southern entrance, 2 km/1.25 mi from the turnoff, tel. 998/874-5170, www.casacenote.com, 8 A.M.–9 P.M. daily, US$5–15) has a breezy patio dining area just steps from the sea's edge. You can order beach food such as quesadillas or a guacamole plate, or something heftier—the seafood is always tasty and fresh. Every Sunday at noon the hotel hosts an awesome Texas-style barbecue (US$15) that is popular with expats up and down the Riviera Maya.

Worth treating yourself, the **Blue Sky**

(Blue Sky Hotel, southern entrance, 1.7 km/1 mi from the turnoff, tel. 984/801-4004, 8–10 A.M., noon–4 P.M., and 4–10 P.M. daily, US$5–24) offers delicious Italian and Mexican specialties. Dishes are prepared to order and the presentation is beautiful—try the grilled calamari with vegetables, a simple meal that you'll remember long after you've gone home. With only a handful of tables, this is a perfect place for an intimate dinner. Just be sure to call for a reservation or arrive early.

INFORMATION AND SERVICES

There are no formal services here because it's not really a formal town. Head to Tulum for ATMs, medical services, Internet, groceries, and more.

GETTING THERE AND AROUND

The turnoff to the southern portion of Tankah Tres is between Kms. 237 and 238 on the main highway, and marked with a large road sign. Driving south from Cancún, you'll have to overshoot the entrance a short distance until a break in the median (at Dreams Resort) allows you to make a U-turn and return to the turnoff; the access road to the northern section is a bit further and is marked with a large sign for Oscar y Lalo's. From the southern turnoff, the access road makes a bee-line for the shore, then turns abruptly to the left, hugging the beach and passing the listed hotels and sights. If you don't have a car, you can ask a *combi* to drop you at the turnoff, but they do not enter Tankah Tres itself.

www.moon.com

DESTINATIONS | ACTIVITIES | BLOGS | MAPS | BOOKS

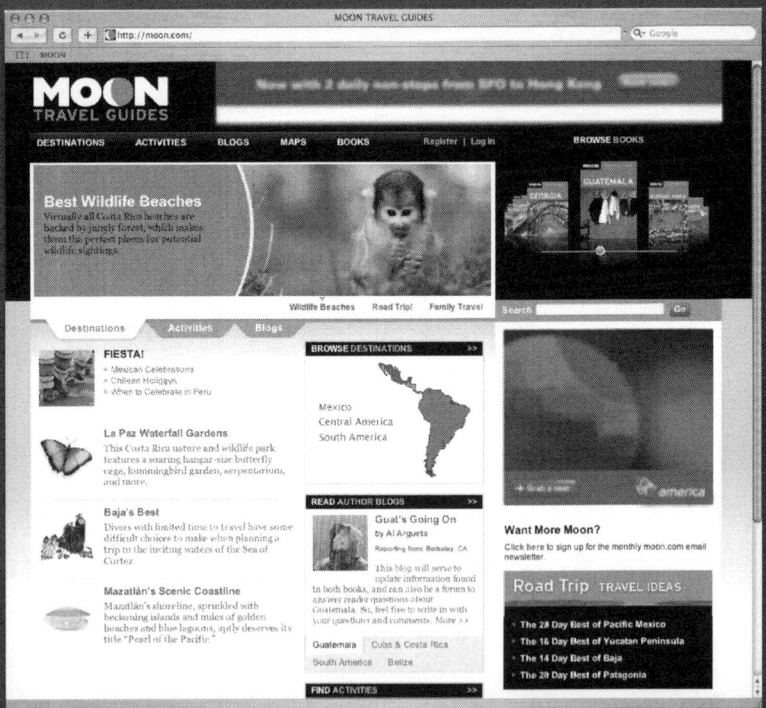

MOON.COM is all new, and ready to help plan your next trip! Filled with fresh trip ideas and strategies, author interviews, informative blogs, a detailed map library, and descriptions of all the Moon guidebooks, Moon.com is all you need to get out and explore the world—or even places in your own backyard. As always, when you travel with Moon, expect an experience that is uncommon and truly unique.

MAP SYMBOLS

▦ Expressway	**⟨** Highlight	✕ Airfield	⚓ Golf Course
Primary Road	○ City/Town	✈ Airport	▯ Parking Area
Secondary Road	◉ State Capital	▲ Mountain	▲ Archaeological Site
▭▭▭ Unpaved Road	⊛ National Capital	✦ Unique Natural Feature	▮ Church
- - - - - Trail	★ Point of Interest		▮ Gas Station
············· Ferry	• Accommodation	⦚ Waterfall	⬯ Glacier
⊷⊷⊷ Railroad	▼ Restaurant/Bar	▲ Park	Mangrove
▦ Pedestrian Walkway	▪ Other Location	⬗ Trailhead	Reef
⫿⫿⫿ Stairs	Λ Campground	⛷ Skiing Area	▱ Swamp

CONVERSION TABLES

°C = (°F - 32) / 1.8
°F = (°C x 1.8) + 32
1 inch = 2.54 centimeters (cm)
1 foot = 0.304 meters (m)
1 yard = 0.914 meters
1 mile = 1.6093 kilometers (km)
1 km = 0.6214 miles
1 fathom = 1.8288 m
1 chain = 20.1168 m
1 furlong = 201.168 m
1 acre = 0.4047 hectares
1 sq km = 100 hectares
1 sq mile = 2.59 square km
1 ounce = 28.35 grams
1 pound = 0.4536 kilograms
1 short ton = 0.90718 metric ton
1 short ton = 2,000 pounds
1 long ton = 1.016 metric tons
1 long ton = 2,240 pounds
1 metric ton = 1,000 kilograms
1 quart = 0.94635 liters
1 US gallon = 3.7854 liters
1 Imperial gallon = 4.5459 liters
1 nautical mile = 1.852 km

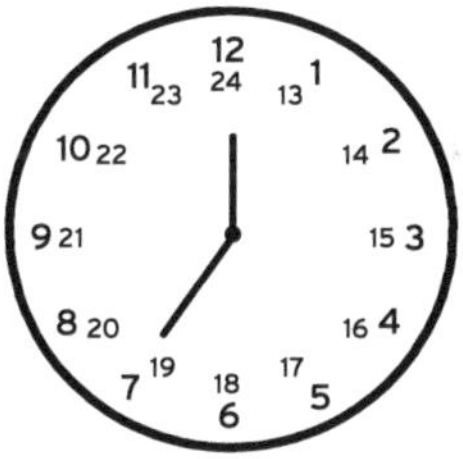

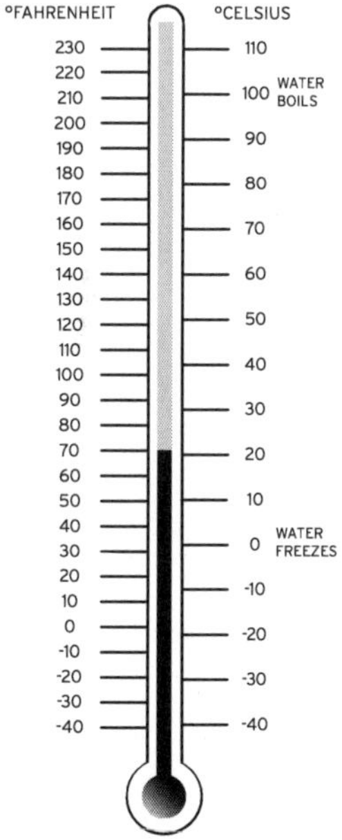

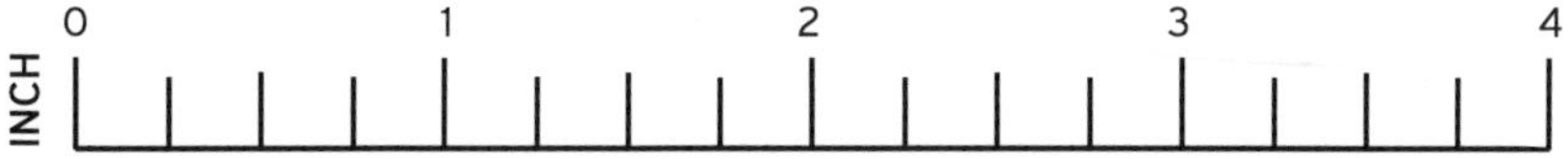

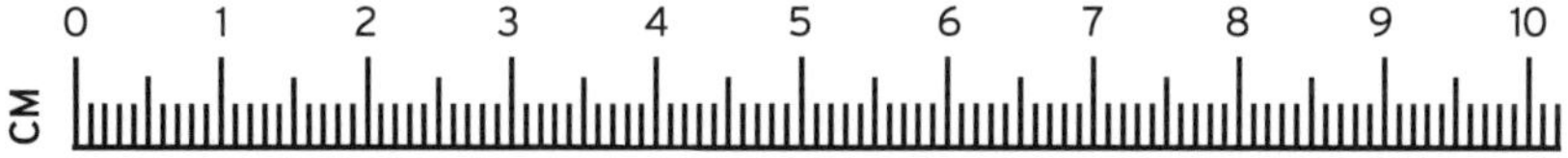

MOON COZUMEL & THE RIVIERA MAYA
Avalon Travel
a member of the Perseus Books Group
1700 Fourth Street
Berkeley, CA 94710, USA
www.moon.com

Editor: Sabrina Young
Series Manager: Kathryn Ettinger
Copy Editor: Amy Scott
Graphics Coordinator: Tabitha Lahr
Production Coordinator: Tabitha Lahr
Cover Designer: Kathryn Osgood
Map Editor: Brice Ticen
Cartographers: Chris Markiewicz and Kat Bennett

ISBN: 978-1-59880-335-8

Front cover photo: © Kim Bunker/istockphoto.com
Title page photo: beach on Isla Cozumel's east side
© Liza Prado

Printed in the United States

ABOUT THE AUTHORS

Liza Prado

Liza Prado was working as a corporate attorney in San Francisco when she decided to take a leap of faith and try travel writing and photography. Seven years later, she has coauthored 11 guidebooks and written numerous feature stories and travel blogs to destinations in Latin America and the Caribbean. Her photographs have been featured in various guidebooks and on travel websites such as Home&Abroad and Away.com.

Since her first visit to the region a decade ago, the Yucatán has remained one of Liza's favorite places to travel. While researching this guide, she dived along coral reefs, snorkeled through cenotes, clambered on Maya ruins, paddled through mangroves, spied monkeys and tropical birds, and explored colonial cities and cobblestone towns (not to mention a nightclub or two) – all with a toddler in tow.

A graduate of Brown University and Stanford Law School, Liza currently lives in San Cristóbal de las Casas, Mexico with her husband and frequent coauthor Gary Chandler, and their daughter Eva Quetzal.

Gary Chandler

Gary Chandler grew up in a small ski town south of Lake Tahoe, CA. He earned his bachelor's degree at UC Berkeley and spent a year abroad in Mexico City and Oaxaca. After graduation, Gary backpacked through much of Mexico and Central America, and later through Southeast Asia, Europe, and the Caribbean. His first guidebook assignment was covering the highlands of Guatemala, followed by assignments in El Salvador, Honduras, Mexico, Brazil, the Dominican Republic, and elsewhere.

Gary has contributed to more than twenty guidebooks in all, many coauthored with wife and fellow travel writer/photographer Liza Prado. The ninth edition of their *Moon Yucatán Peninsula* guidebook received a Journey Award for "Best Guide Book" from *Adventure Journey Magazine* in 2007. Between assignments, Gary has earned a masters degree in journalism at Columbia University, worked as a newspaper and radio reporter, and published numerous articles and blogs about travel in Latin America.

Printed in Great Britain
by Amazon.co.uk, Ltd.,
Marston Gate.